Ebenezer Morgan

Christ at the Well

Devotional Studies in the Fourth Chapter of the Fourth Gospel

Ebenezer Morgan

Christ at the Well
Devotional Studies in the Fourth Chapter of the Fourth Gospel

ISBN/EAN: 9783337026622

Printed in Europe, USA, Canada, Australia, Japan

Cover: Foto ©Lupo / pixelio.de

More available books at **www.hansebooks.com**

DEVOTIONAL STUDIES IN THE
FOURTH CHAPTER OF THE FOURTH GOSPEL.

BY THE REV.

EBENEZER MORGAN.

𝕷𝖔𝖓𝖉𝖔𝖓:
CHARLES H. KELLY,
2 CASTLE ST., CITY RD.; AND PATERNOSTER ROW, E.C.

𝕭𝖎𝖗𝖒𝖎𝖓𝖌𝖍𝖆𝖒:
MIDLAND EDUCATIONAL CO.
1897.

PRINTED BY
MORRISON AND GIBB LIMITED,
EDINBURGH.

TO MY BROTHER,

THE REV. JOHN HUGH MORGAN.

Preface.

———◇———

THESE short studies are published with the hope of rendering help to the vast company of Bible Students, Lay Preachers, and Sunday-School Teachers in their sacred toil; and of throwing some light on one of the most instructive, interesting, and beautiful incidents in the life of our Lord. They are sent forth with fervent prayer for the blessing of Him without whose Holy Spirit nothing is wise or good.

Contents.

I.

Leisure Nobly Employed.

Leisure is the time for doing something useful: this leisure the diligent man will obtain, the lazy man never.—BENJAMIN FRANKLIN.

The bits of wayside work are very sweet. Perhaps the odd bits, when all is done, will really come to more than the seemingly greater pieces.—Miss HAVERGAL.

Leisure Nobly Employed.

"Jesus therefore, being wearied with His journey, sat thus on the well."—ST. JOHN iv. 6.

IT is not stated by the Evangelist how far Christ had travelled that day. If from Jerusalem, it was a long and tedious journey, a distance of about thirty-four miles. When we remember that the climate was tropical, and the time of day was noontide, no wonder that the Man Christ Jesus should desire to rest. It is probable that He had struggled hard with thirst, hunger, and fatigue, that He might reach a resting-place where the associations were so historic, and the natural scenery was so lovely.

In coming from the south, Christ and His disciples crossed the wild and rugged Ephraim range of hills; when they stood on Mount

Gerizim, there lay before them a landscape of
more than ordinary beauty. Dr. Smith, in his
Bible Dictionary, says that "travellers vie with
each other in the language which they employ to
describe the scene that bursts here so suddenly
upon them, on arriving in spring or early summer
at this Paradise of the Holy Land." Dr. Robin-
son tells us that "the whole valley was filled with
gardens of vegetables, and orchards of all kinds
of fruits, watered by fountains which burst forth
in various parts, and flow westwards in refreshing
streams. It came upon us suddenly, like a scene
of fairy enchantment. We saw nothing to com-
pare with it in all Palestine." Startling as was
the change, from the romantic ruggedness of the
mountains to the quiet and bewitching loveliness
of the valley, it was only typical of the transition
in the actual circumstances of our Lord's life.
He had been in the City of Jerusalem, and His
ministry had been accompanied with demonstrations of success and triumph. Large numbers
came to Him as candidates for baptism ; and on
the great day of the Feast, when they saw the
miracles which He performed, many believed on
His name. In reading the narrative of His busy

and exciting life in the city, the immense stir He
created by His words and deeds, we feel a reverent
awe, as in the presence of a majestic and omni-
potent Being; and the impression lingers in the
mind until suddenly we come upon this scene by
the well, which is so pathetic in its revelation of
the human aspect of our Lord's character.

The great lesson we learn from this incident
is, that

JESUS MADE A MOST SACRED USE OF LEISURE.

No one ever crowded so much patient, earnest
and loving toil into such a short space of time.
His work was never done in a mechanical or
perfunctory manner. He always acted, in whatever He undertook, with whole-hearted intensity
of devotion, so that He needed occasional intervals of repose. But He was never really
unemployed. His leisure meant no "masterly
inactivity." If not engaged in doing good to
man, His mind was occupied in calm and holy
communion with His Father.

When the infants were brought to Him for His
benediction, the disciples forbade them. Why?
Do not think that they were so hard-hearted

2

as to have no spark of sympathy with the children. Nothing of the kind. Our Saviour would not have called such men to be His apostles. What led them to act as they did was, not antipathy to the little ones, but thoughtful and tender regard for their Master: it was their desire that, tired as He must have been with the activities of the day, He should now enjoy undisturbed quiet and freedom from intrusion and annoyance. But His intense love for young life was more potent than the longing for rest. Hence those beautiful words, " Suffer the little children to come unto Me, and forbid them not: for of such is the kingdom of God " (St. Mark x. 14).

On another memorable occasion, when He was weary with incessant labour and had no leisure so much as to eat, in order to escape the crush and clamour of the crowd He invited His followers to retire with Him to some quiet retreat. " Come ye yourselves apart into a desert place, and rest awhile." They went by ship privately ; but they were observed by the populace, who walked on foot along the coast of the Lake of Galilee to the place where they landed ; and when He saw the multitude, to Him they were "as sheep without a shepherd"; and although the disciples were anxious that He should enjoy seclusion, and said, "Send them away," He fed the hungry throng, and taught them many heavenly truths. He illustrated constantly in His life the precept He gave to His disciples after feeding the five thousand with five loaves and two fishes: "Gather up the broken pieces that remain over, that nothing be lost" (St. John vi. 12 R.V.).

In the economising of passing moments He has given us an example worthy of imitation. Life divides itself into two great departments of labour and rest. There is a time for work and there is a time for repose, and between the toil of the day and the sleep of the night there should be an interval of leisure. No man can stand the strain of uninterrupted labour. Mind and body cry out for relief and recreation. Cervantes says, "For the bow cannot possibly stand always bent, nor can human nature or human frailty subsist without some lawful recreation." There is a touching legend of the Apostle John illustrative of this truth. In his old age he used to find pleasure in the attachment of a tamed partridge. One day, as he held it in his bosom and was gently stroking it, a huntsman suddenly approached, and wondering that one so illustrious should take to so trivial an amusement, he asked, " Art thou that John whose singular renown has inspired even me with a great desire to know thee? How, then, canst thou occupy thyself with an employment so humble?" The apostle replied, "What is that in thy hand?" He answered, "A bow." "And why dost thou not always carry it bent?" "Because," he answered, "it would in that case lose its strength; and when it was necessary to shoot, it would fail, from the too continuous tension." "Then let not this slight and brief relaxation of mine perplex thee," answered the apostle, "since without it the spirit would flag from the unremitted strain, and fail when the call of duty came." This legend contains a fund of philosophy, and it has its appropriate lesson for us who live in these times of strenuous exertion. In the world, how keen is the strife of commercial competition, how eager and intense is the race for riches, position, and fame! In the Church, organisations and activities are so multiplied, and the demands upon our time, thought, and energy are so numerous, pressing, and incessant, that we

are in danger of forgetting that if we do bend the
bow constantly, it will break or lose its strength ;
and that if we wish to preserve it in unimpaired
force, the tension must be relieved now and then
by loosening the strings. In the busy career let
there be occasional intervals of physical and
mental rest, and of innocent recreation. What
are we doing in our moments or hours of leisure ?
Released from the stern and imperative claims of
duty, and at perfect liberty to go where we like
and do what we please, what are the forces which
attract us ? Are they the frivolous and the
sensual ? or are they the intellectual and spiritual ?
Of Peter and John it is said that, when they were
emancipated from the authority of the Sanhedrin,
" being let go, they went to their own company."
Tell me how a man conducts himself in those
seasons of unfettered freedom, in the evening of
each day, the Sabbath of each week, the holidays
of each year by the seaside or amongst sylvan
glens and mountain lakes, and you supply me
with a decisive test of character. Amid the joy
of liberty genuine Christians will not forget their
vows of lifelong loyalty and service ; they will not
lose sight of the fact that they are always and

everywhere His ; that in a spiritual sense they can
never be off duty. When they who bear His
name know how to use their leisure for His glory
and the good of their fellows, the prospect will
brighten for the day when there shall be

> One God, one law, one element,
> And one far-off divine event,
> To which the whole creation moves.

As the goldsmith gathers up every particle of
the gold-dust, so we should redeem every moment,
even those erroneously called the spare minutes.
It is said that a carpet from the San Francisco
Mint was burnt some years ago, and yielded
£505 worth of gold-dust, which had fallen in
imperceptible particles during the course of five
years. Time is more precious than gold. Wealth,
once lost, may be recovered by industry and per-
severance; health, once lost, may be regained by
care and medical skill ; but time, once squandered,
can never be recalled. Dryden says—

> Not Heaven itself upon the past has power
> For what has been, has been, and I have had my hour.

Many have carved for themselves a niche in the
temple of fame through the diligent use of odd

moments. Bishop Wilberforce sometimes wrote a sermon, to be preached next day before the Queen, while travelling by night in a carriage attached to a luggage train. Elihu Burritt mastered eighteen ancient and two - and - twenty modern languages at intervals when his attention was not demanded at the forge. Sir Roderick Murchison assures us that one of the best geologists and botanists he ever knew was a working baker, who, when his bread was taken from the oven, used to go out and hunt for plants and fossils. Sir Joseph Paxton sketched the design of the Crystal Palace on a sheet of blotting-paper one day while waiting at a railway station.

Let our leisure then be consecrated to the noblest ends—

> Take my moments and my days,
> Let them flow in ceaseless praise.

Do good by all means, in stated places and at fixed times, but the Divine life should never be hindered in its spontaneous growth by the fear of speaking "out of season." In the homely wellside talks of life let us try to utter a message of comfort and hope, and the word "fitly spoken" will not be less potent because the speaker or messenger was unconventional in dress or unprofessional in the tones of his voice. "Blessed are ye that sow beside all waters" (Isa. xxxii. 20).

A Woman of Samaria.

Whatever position woman holds in civilised society is clearly a fruit of Christianity.— LORING BRACE, in *Gesta Christi*.

𝕬 𝖂oman of 𝕾amaria.

"There cometh a woman of Samaria to draw water."—St.
John iv. 7.

IN the East it was the custom for the women
to draw the water from the wells. On the
earliest pages of biblical history we read of
"Rebekah the daughter of Bethuel, the son of
Nahor," who was a damsel "fair to look upon,"
meeting Abraham's trusted servant at a well
outside the city of Haran, and affording refreshment both for himself and his camels. In a
country where wells are greatly needed because
of the comparative absence of rain, they are highly
prized, and become the favourite resort of weary
travellers.

As the human Christ was parched with thirst
and had no pitcher wherewith to draw, it was a

happy circumstance that this woman should appear at the right moment with her waterpot to help Him in His need. For some reason or other her name is not given—if it were known at all to the Evangelist. Legend says that it was Photina. Although her name is not mentioned in the sacred narrative, in her interview with Jesus she not only received the light and grace of salvation, but through her association with the Eternal Son of God her memory was made immortal. We learn

I. Jesus knew how to Appreciate one Human Being.

Popular orators are often largely dependent for their inspiration upon the numbers and enthusiasm of their auditors. Before a large and attentive crowd they are borne aloft on the wings of sympathy, sometimes to extraordinary flights of imagination and eloquence. The philosophic teacher can do better with a select and intellectual few. On several occasions Jesus addressed immense throngs on the mount and by the sea. He could adapt Himself to the necessities and exigencies of a promiscuous assembly, and "the common people heard him gladly" (Mark xii. 37).

But it was not always to vast masses He spoke. He was dependent upon no external circumstance for inspiration. That He had *within* Him.

It is an interesting and instructive fact that there are two instances, closely related to each other, of His preaching sublime discourses to single individuals: the one in the case of Nicodemus, who came to Him by night; the other, of the woman whom He met at the well at midday. So impartial was He in the communication of Divine truth, that it would be difficult, if not impossible, to tell which sermon is the more excellent—the one delivered to the poor Samaritan woman, or the one to the rich Jewish ruler.

For the ministry that has occasionally only one hearer there is a compensating advantage. In the application of the truth there is a personal directness which cannot admit of any misunderstanding. There can be no attempt at evading responsibility by shifting it on to the shoulders of others. The conventional hearer of the Gospel often listens for someone else, and thinks the remarks and exhortations of the preacher suitable for his fellow-worshippers, and says, mentally, when any sin or failing is the subject of pulpit rebuke, "That will do for So-and-so: the cap fits, let him wear it." Such a spirit of hearing was not possible in the case before us. There the woman stood alone with Him who knew the secrets of her heart and life, and His word went right home to her conscience, like an arrow to its mark.

Where is the appraiser who can fix the exact value of one soul? It is a jewel of priceless worth.

> Knowest thou the importance of the soul immortal?
> Behold the sky's midnight glory, worlds on worlds:
> One thousand add, and twice ten thousand more,
> Then weigh them all,—one soul outweighs them all.

No one knows its intrinsic and relative preciousness so well as He who gave His life as the price of its redemption, and no one knows so well as He the beneficent possibilities and results which may attend the conversion of one sinner. In the early part of his career Dr. Lyman Beecher once engaged to preach for a brother minister whose church was in a remote district, peopled by a sparse and scattered population. It was in midwinter, the day was unusually stormy and cold, and the snow lay so deep in some places that he could scarcely proceed. On his arrival, although he saw no one, he took his seat in the pulpit. Presently one man came in and sat down, and at the appointed hour the preacher began. The service was closed with the benediction, when the solitary hearer departed and left the preacher alone. Twenty years afterward, Dr. Beecher was travelling in Ohio when a stranger accosted him by name, and, much to his surprise, said they had once spent two hours together in a house alone in a storm. " Do you remember preaching," said he, " twenty years ago, to one man?" " Yes, yes," said the doctor, grasping his hand, "that I do ; and if you are the man, I have been wishing to see you ever since." " I am the man," was the reply ; " and that sermon saved my soul, made a minister of me, and yonder is my church. The converts of that sermon, sir, are all over Ohio." As the Saviour sat by the well, no doubt the uppermost feeling in His heart was an intense desire that all the inhabitants of Sychar should experience the blessedness of the great salvation which He alone could impart. That was the end of His wishes, His prayers, His self-denials. How was

it accomplished? Not by going up into the
Temple on Mount Gerizim at the hour of service
and proclaiming the truths of the Gospel to those
who were assembled, nor by publishing them in
the open air in the streets of the city of Sychar,
but by the concentration of His love and sympathy
upon one person. What is the result? Through
the woman's agency others are affected and saved.
We read, " Many of the Samaritans of that city
believed on Him for the saying of the woman "
(St. John iv. 39). This is the Divinely-appointed
method. They who are illumined by His light
and fired by His love are to be centres of moral
radiance and sources of moral heat to those who
are in the darkness of sin and the desolation of
unbelief—

> Heaven doth with us as we with torches do,
> Not light them for themselves.

The time will come when people will be con-
verted by hundreds and thousands. If we desire
to see the dawn of that glorious day, let us care
for the one, let us fix our thought and prayer
upon a single individual, and it may be that in
due time he will be a messenger to the multitude.

Another lesson we learn is this, that

II. JESUS ACTED AS WOMAN'S FRIEND AND UPLIFTER.

The current maxims of Jewish society were : " Never speak to a woman in the street, even if she be thy wife." " Burn the words of the Law rather than teach them to a woman." Her sex forbade a Rabbi to hold unnecessary converse with her. The Scribes and Pharisees treated her with contempt, and held it a crime to look on an unveiled woman in public ; they gathered up their robes in the streets and in the synagogues lest they should touch her. Mahomet denies that woman has a soul. To us, who live in a land more or less under the influence of Christian civilisation, all this sounds strangely false. Our Master honoured woman, and suffered one, out of whom he had cast seven devils, to minister unto Him.

In the animal world the female sex is treated with consideration. There is a kind of chivalry among birds and beasts. If we find respect for the weaker sex in the realm of animal life, surely we should expect to find it in the region of human

3

intelligence. You can gauge the measure of national progress in any country by the way in which woman is treated. Canning says, " To raise the weaker sex in self-respect as well as in the esteem of the stronger, is the first step from barbarism to civilisation." This is a criterion of morals, and an evidence of the influence of religion. In those lands where superstitions and idolatries abound she is a debased slave, but where Christ is honoured she is raised to her rightful position as man's helpmeet, his intelligent and sympathetic companion. There is no need to bring out a woman's edition of the Bible. We have it already. A Hindu woman once said to a missionary, "Surely your Bible was written by a woman?" " Why? " " Because it says so many kind things for women. Our pundits never refer to us but in reproach."

Further, this woman of Samaria was a sinner. Christ laid His hands gently upon that part of her life which she would fain hope was un-known to Him, being strangers to each other ; but in this she was mistaken, and He speedily showed to her that He knew all when He said, " Thou hast had five husbands, and he whom thou

hast is not thy husband; in that saidst thou truly."
Ingenious interpreters of the Bible will always be
able to discover curious and strange analogies,
and some have taken the "five husbands" to
represent the five religions brought to Samaria by
colonists from Assyria. They were from Babylon,
Cuthah, Ava, Hamath, Sepharvaim; but this
narrative is not an allegory or a fiction: it is
authentic history, a relation of facts.

She had lived in a state of open defiance of the
restraints of religion and the canons of morality.
She had lost that which constitutes the charm and
glory of womanhood—purity of life. This gone
all is gone.

If the sanctimonious Pharisees looked down
with contempt upon her because of her sex, their
disdain was not diminished by the fact of her
laxity of life. They turned away from her with
disgust. But Jesus has changed the attitude of
the world not only towards women, but also
towards notorious sinners, irrespective of sex.
He said, "I come not to call the righteous, but
sinners, to repentance" (Mark ii. 17). He had
limitless faith in human nature, even in its most
degraded forms. Science discovers utility in

waste, and beauty in dust and dirt. Ruskin finds the elements of a crystal in a handful of mud. A lady, examining one of Turner's pictures, remarked, "But I do not see these things in nature." "Madam," replied the artist, "don't you wish you did?" The eye of Christ, as it rested on this sinful woman, saw in her the possibility of saintliness.

The age when Christ came was weighed down with gloomy pessimism. He gives hope to the despairing, and offers purity to the worst. This woman found it to be so. As she looked upon Him she found in the revelation of His love the promise and potency for renewal of nature, reformation of conduct, and holiness of life; for from His face there streamed into her benighted soul the sunlight of hope, dispelling the gloom of her despondency, and filling her heart with a new joy.

III.

The Son of Man.

Thou seemest human and Divine,
The highest, holiest manhood, Thou.

TENNYSON.

ᛏᚺᛖ Son of Man.

"Jesus saith unto her, Give Me to drink."—ST. JOHN iv. 7.

IN this phrase, "Jesus saith," we have the distinguishing characteristic of the Fourth Gospel. Whereas the Synoptists relate more particularly the deeds of the Messiah, John narrates His words. They tell us what he did, John reports more fully what He said. His discourses and dialogues are as precious in their significance, and as striking a proof of His Divinity, as His miracles, for "never man spake like this man" (St. John vii. 46).

This is one of the seven sayings He uttered to the Samaritan woman. With the Jews, seven was looked upon as the number of completion. In the old Testament we read of seven days being occupied in the Creation; in the Jewish calendar every seventh year was a Sabbath, and seven times seventy years a Jubilee. The three great Jewish feasts lasted seven days, and between the first and second of these feasts were seven weeks. In the New Testament it is frequently used, and especially in the Book of the Revelation, where we read of the seven churches of Asia, the seven candlesticks, the seven stars, the seven trumpets, the seven vials, the seven horns, the seven spirits before the throne. It is a singular coincidence that this number is found so often in the ministry of Jesus. He delivered seven Beatitudes in His Sermon on the Mount, inserted seven divisions in the Lord's Prayer, and uttered seven sayings from the Cross. In the case of the Samaritan woman He spoke, whilst the conversation lasted, seven times, and the words of the text were the first He uttered. "Jesus saith unto her, Give Me to drink." We observe

I. *THAT JESUS, AS HUMAN, WAS SUBJECT TO PHYSICAL INFIRMITIES.*

In the three Epistles, St. John shows that the Son of God appeared in human form. In the

Gospel it is seen that He who thus stooped to the limitations of our humanity was no other than God. The Epistles dilate upon the reality of His Incarnation, the Gospel dwells more fully upon His Divinity. In the early Church it was believed that St. John wrote his Gospel in opposition to the tenets of Cerinthus, an Ephesian who was a contemporary of "the disciple whom Jesus loved." Tradition says that one day, as the apostle was entering the public bath at Ephesus, he learned that the heretic was within. Immediately he sprang from the place, exclaiming, " Let us flee lest the house fall upon us, since Cerinthus, the enemy of truth, is within." Jeremy Taylor says that possibly the premonition was conveyed by prophetic intuition, for immediately upon his retreat the bath fell down and crushed Cerinthus in its ruins. Can you not understand the apostle of love becoming a veritable Boanerges in refuting the heresy which denied the Divinity of his Lord ? The very first verse in his Gospel is like a thunderbolt hurled into the enemy's camp. " In the beginning was the Word, and the Word was with God, and the Word was God " (St. John i. 1). Cerinthus was the pioneer of a long pro-

cession of able men, such as Arius and Socinus,
who accepted the same heresy with sundry
modifications. On the other hand, John had to
deal with a certain Gnostic sect, the Docetæ, who
regarded the humanity of Christ as a semblance,
and not as a reality. They maintained that it
was impossible to conceive of the union of the
Divine Being with a body composed of matter,
which they held to be the seat of evil. To this
curious and yet dangerous heresy we have a
strong and sufficient answer in the text. If His
humanity were but a phantasm or an illusion,
would He have experienced the sensations of
thirst? "Jesus saith unto her, Give Me to drink."
If He were only a phantasm would He have felt
the pain and the power of temptation? The
scene in the desert, where He was brought into
conflict with the devil, shows that He took upon
Him our nature in its liability both to physical
weakness and spiritual struggle. If He were only
a phantasm would He have experienced the agony
of desertion and the shame of derision, when His
love was requited by hatred on the part of those
upon whom He had sought to pour the light of
heavenly grace and truth? If this theory were

correct, the nails were not driven through His hands and feet, the spear of the Roman soldier never pierced His side, He was never crucified or buried, He is not risen, He is not in heaven in bodily form. Such an improbable hypothesis refutes itself by its absurdity. He had a true body and a reasonable soul. He possessed human faculties, performed human acts, and although sinless He laboured under the infirmities of human nature. In his prophecy Daniel calls Him "the Son of man." In the Gospels this title is applied to Him eighty-four times. It occurs thirty-two times in St. Matthew, fourteen times in St. Mark, twenty-six times in St. John. It is noteworthy that Christ claims this appellation for Himself; and it is never used by His disciples except in the case of the proto-martyr Stephen, whose eye of faith was not blinded by the shower of stones, for he saw "the Son of man standing at the right hand of God," as if waiting to receive him. It is only employed by Christ in regard to Himself; and although the title is suggestive of frailty, the context of the passages in which it is used shows that, in submitting to the humiliation and

poverty of His earthly life, He had not abrogated
the functions of dignity, authority, and beneficence
peculiar to the Godhead. " The Son of man is
Lord also of the Sabbath " (St. Mark ii. 28).
" The Son of man hath power on earth to forgive
sins " (St. Mark ii. 10). " The Son of man is
come to seek and to save that which was lost "
(St. Luke xix. 10). The Eutychians, who
flourished in the fifth century, believed that He
was entirely God previous to the Incarnation, and
entirely man during His sojourn on earth. We
hold that He was God and man at the same time,
i.e. He did not cease to be Divine when He
became human. He who was upheld in the arms
of Mary was the Sustainer of all things. He
who sat thus on the well, wearied with His journey,
was " the Creator of the ends of the earth, who
fainteth not, neither is weary." He who said to
the woman, " Give Me to drink," " sendeth the
springs into the valleys which run among the
hills." Do not ask me to explain the manner in
which He was able to do this. If we cannot
understand the union between body and soul in
ourselves, much less can we comprehend the
union of the Divine and human in Christ. We

are now in thought under the shadow of the most impressive, sublime, and incomprehensible truth in our belief. "And, without controversy, great is the mystery of godliness: God was manifest in the flesh" (Tim. iii. 16).

There is, however, an aspect of the Incarnation which makes its appeal to our rational faculty. Its *raison d'être* is to be found in the wisdom of the Divine mind, in the boundless love of the Divine heart. With our finite intellect we are unable to realise what God is in His essence. He appeared in human form that He might come into sympathetic touch with us in our needs and struggles; that He might supply us with a pattern of purity, an example worthy of imitation; and that He might demonstrate His compassion, both by His unselfish life and atoning death. He lived, suffered, and died in our nature. Whenever we think of Him and the beneficent mystery of His Person, let us do so, not in a spirit of curious and irreverent speculation, but with subdued awe and grateful love.

He is "the Son of man" not only in the sense that He participated in our weakness, but also that He was the representative and archetype of the new humanity. And this leads us to note

II. THAT HE IGNORED RACIAL JEALOUSIES.

Angry feuds between communities, as between individuals, are often found, when traced to their origin, to have sprung from trivial causes. "Behold how much wood (marg., How great a forest) is kindled by how small a fire" (Jas. iii. 5, R.V.). In the 4th chapter of the Book of Ezra there is a graphic account of the rise of the controversy between the Jews and the Samaritans. Upon their return from Babylonian captivity the former began to rebuild the Temple at Jerusalem. An application was made by the Cuthæans that they might assist, but the request was refused by Zerubbabel and the elders, because the Cuthæans or Samaritans were not of the seed of Abraham, and they mingled idolatry with the worship of God. Whereupon they determined, in the bitterness of their chagrin, that if they could not help they would hinder, and for some time they pursued a system of obstruction. They annoyed the Jews, and delayed the work of rebuilding to such an extent that they were compelled to wield the sword as well as the trowel. At last there came a crisis. Manasseh, who was of the priestly lineage, was condemned and expelled by Nehemiah for his matrimonial alliance with the daughter of Sanballat, the governor of Samaria. Now the fury of the Samaritans was so intense that they decided to build a rival temple on Mount Gerizim, with Manasseh as their first high-priest. We need not dwell any further upon the history of this alienation. Suffice it to state that time did not heal the old feud. It was there when Christ came, and as bitter as ever. He did not, however, allow it to be any barrier to His work of mercy. His love refused to be circumscribed by the limits of any national animosity. As a rule, when there has been a quarrel between two parties, the nobler of the two is the first to make advances towards reconciliation. Jesus went into the country of the Samaritans, and this no ordinary Jew would do. If the Jew wished to go from Judea to Galilee, he would travel along a most circuitous route in order to avoid touching the soil of Samaria. Not so does Jesus act. He does not take the roundabout way, *i.e.* crossing the Jordan to the north of the Dead Sea, and going along the land of Peræa, and recrossing the Jordan into Galilee to the south of the Lake of Tiberias. He takes the most direct and convenient road; and, in fact, what to others was repulsive, to Him was attractive. He is drawn to it by a magnetic and irresistible spell. " He must needs go through Samaria " (ver. 4).

Observe that the first to speak was not the woman, but Jesus ; and she was astonished to find that a Jew should have the courage to set at naught the restrictions of caste. " How is it that thou, being a Jew, askest drink of me, who am a woman of Samaria ? for the Jews have no dealings with the Samaritans " (ver. 9).

If the proud Hebrew did regard his Samaritan neighbour with disdain, Jesus never did. In Him the weak and helpless have always found a Friend, and despised and oppressed nationalities a generous and fearless Champion. He never uttered such harsh denunciation and censure to the Samaritans as He did to the Jews. For them He had words of love and sympathy. We need only mention two or three instances.

(a) John and James asked Him to command fire from heaven to consume the inhabitants of

the Samaritan village, who had declined to receive
them. His disciples are vindictive, while the
Master is magnanimous in His tolerance and
tenderness (St. Luke ix. 54, 55).

(*b*) Ten lepers are cleansed: only one returns
to express his gratitude, "and he was a Samaritan"
(St. Luke xvii. 15–19).

(*c*) In the parable of the unfortunate man who
had fallen among thieves on his way from
Jerusalem to Jericho, who acted the part of the
neighbour? It was not the priest and the Levite
—they passed by on the other side. It was he who
bound up his bruises, pouring in oil and wine,
set him on his own beast, and brought him to an
inn, and paid for his entertainment. It was the
Samaritan. Henceforth that name which was so
much hated by the Jews becomes a synonym for
noble sympathy and generous benevolence—a
name for the Son of God Himself, for He is "the
Good Samaritan" (St. Luke x. 30–37).

Have nations to-day their antipathies, races
their prejudices, and sects their bigotries? However deep-seated, they are not insuperable obstacles
to the world's evangelisation. Let us copy the
example of Jesus, and permit no conventional

4

distinctions to check the flow of charity and beneficence. He bids us to go forth and win all men to His feet. He gives us a commission which includes in the range of its influence "all nations." He says to us to-day, "Preach the Gospel to every creature, high and low, rich and poor ; tell them of the love of God, which is unsectarian, cosmopolitan, and infinite."

IV

The Gift of God.

God often visits us, but most of the time we are not at home.—JOSEPH ROUX.

God has been pleased to prescribe limits to His own power, and to work out His ends within these limits.—PALEY.

𝕮𝖍𝖊 𝕲𝖎𝖋𝖙 of 𝕲𝖔𝖉.

"If thou knewest the gift of God, and who it is that saith
to thee, Give Me to drink; thou wouldest have asked of
Him, and He would have given thee living water."—
ST. JOHN iv. 10.

THE reply which the woman of Samaria
gave to the natural request of the thirsty
Traveller for a cooling draught from Sychar's
Well, is characterised by what Dr. Plummer calls
"feminine pertness." If she did not bluntly refuse
the request, it was not granted with any of that
grace which is so peculiarly woman's property.

The common instincts of humanity and kind-
ness might have prompted her to offer a refreshing draught, so that the pangs of thirst in any
stranger, irrespective of his nationality, might be
assuaged. How does Jesus deal with her after

this exhibition of "pertness"? Does He retort
with words of stern reproof? Does He show any
trace of the spirit of resentment? Her harshness
becomes an occasion for the display of His
patience and tact, and the exercise of the sweetest
courtesy. Nothing could be more beautiful than
the manner in which He draws her attention
from the earthly to the heavenly. His urbanity
stands out in bold relief from her abruptness.
Paraphrased, His answer means this: "Now, I
am the petitioner. I have asked for a simple
favour, at which thou art surprised. Given
spiritual perception on thy part, our positions
would be reversed. In that case thou wouldst
be the petitioner, and thy request for those un-
speakably more precious blessings would be
granted immediately and gladly, and the thirst
of thy soul would be quenched for ever in the
Fountain of Life." We learn

1. THAT A REALISATION OF THE VALUE AND
   NEED OF DIVINE FAVOUR IS ABSOLUTELY
   NECESSARY.

"If thou knewest the gift of God," etc.
The mind of the woman was shrouded by

dense ignorance on two subjects. She was in the dark respecting

(a) *The preciousness and freeness of Salvation.*

The water-carrier goes along the streets of Cairo with his water-skin on his shoulder, crying out, "The Gift of God." The inhabitants of Oriental countries are subject to long spells of dry weather, unrelieved by any refreshing showers. At this very time India is slowly recovering from the effects of famine, brought about mainly through the failure of autumn rains. To the people of the East water stands out as the sign and symbol of the greatest earthly good: its presence denotes health and happiness, its absence or scarcity means disease and death. It was of the material element the woman was thinking when she said, "Sir, give me this water, that I thirst not, neither come hither to draw" (ver. 15); whereas Christ alluded to that which fertilises the sterile, cleanses the corrupt, and refreshes the weary soul—that which is, pre-eminently amid the numberless bestowments of Heaven, "*the* Gift of God." As He sat there by the well He might have repeated the stirring invitation given by the evangelical prophet Isaiah to the people of his

day to participate in the provisions of the Gospel.
How appropriately the words could have fallen
from His lips, "Ho, every one that thirsteth,
come ye to the waters; and he that hath no
money"! (Isa. lv. 1).

What cannot be purchased by the gold of
Ophir, nor merited by any number of good deeds,
may be received by faith. Paul helps us to
understand the meaning of the phrase when he
says that "the gift of God is eternal life, through
Jesus Christ our Lord" (Rom. vi. 23).

> 'Tis Heaven alone that is given away,
> 'Tis only God may be had for the asking.

She was in the dark respecting

(b) *The superhuman rank of Jesus.*

"And who it is that saith unto thee."

As yet He had not supplied her with any proof
of His Divinity, and in His appearance there was
no indication that He was more than an ordinary
Jew. If Mary, who was familiar with him, did
not recognise the identity of the ¿risen Saviour
—who even mistook Him for the gardener, and
only discovered her error by the way in which He
uttered her name; if Peter, who was one of His

companions, neither distinguished His form as He stood on the shore of the Galilean lake on that memorable morning, nor knew His voice when He asked them, " Children, have ye any meat ? "—it is not so singular to find the woman of Samaria utterly insensible to the dignity of the stranger with whom she was conversing. So far no gleam of light has shone on her dark mind. Later on she found out that He was no common traveller. The discovery came with startling suddenness : it came, like a flash of lightning, with the revelation of His knowledge of her life. He whose weary frame was resting by the well must be Omniscient, for He was acquainted with her guilty intimacies, and at the same time references were made by Him to the institution of means and methods for the pardon of sin and the cleansing away of moral defilement.

This is not the only scene in the life of our Lord illustrative of His dual nature. If He suffered from hunger, He fed the five thousand and multiplied the loaves and fishes. If He slept in the boat, He stilled the storm and hushed the tempest into a great calm. If He submitted to

be judged, scourged, and crucified, He demon-
strated His Godhead by His glorious Resurrection.   If the woman of Samaria at first only saw
Him weary, hungry, and thirsty, before long she
had glimpses of His superhuman knowledge and
power.

> There shone through all His fleshly dress
> Bright shoots of everlastingness.

At the moment when He spoke these words,
" If thou knewest," etc., she had not discerned
the signs of His majesty.   It is said that ignorance
is the mother of devotion.   Yes, if by devotion
you mean credulity and superstition.   We are
more inclined to the proverb, that ignorance is
the mother of insolence.   De Bouffiers says
ignorance is prolonged infancy, only deprived of
its charms.   Confucius says that ignorance is a
night of the mind—a night without moon or star.
What Madame Roland said as she bowed to
the Statue of Liberty at the place of execution
can be said of ignorance with equal force and
propriety :

"O Ignorance, what crimes have been com-
mitted in thy name!"

It was this that led the inhabitants of
Jerusalem to reject the message of Jesus ; and
we find Him, in full view of the city, sobbing
forth the tearful and pathetic lament, " If thou
hadst known in this day, even thou, the things
which belong to thy peace ! but now they are hid
from thine eyes " (St. Luke xix. 42, R.V.).

It was this that led the Jews to heap upon
the Innocent One a succession of insults and
reproaches, which reached their culmination in
the agony of Crucifixion. He prayed for His
murderers, " Father, forgive them, for they know
not what they do " (St. Luke xxiii. 34). Whilst
preaching on the Day of Pentecost, Peter fixed
upon this feature of their conduct as a slight
extenuation of their guilt. " And now, brethren,
I wot that through ignorance ye did it, as did
also your rulers " (Acts iii. 17).

It was this that led Saul of Tarsus to persecute
the saints even unto strange cities. When the
scales which had so long blinded his mental
vision were by the mercy of God miraculously
removed from his eyes, he saw that he had pursued a wickedly wrong course of conduct, and
he felt himself to be the chief of sinners.

Nowadays much is said and written on "How to reach the masses," and it is a problem the solution of which demands and deserves our serious thought and practical sympathy. It must be admitted, however, that if the people only realised in any degree the depth of their need, the efficacy of the Gospel, and the infinitude of God's love, they would require no urgent entreaty to come to Him for the pardon, purity, and peace which He alone can give. There is truth, if not poetry, in the well-known lines—

> If all the world my Saviour knew,
> All the world would love Him too.

Oh that we had more of that spiritual knowledge which realises something of the boundless stores of grace treasured in Christ for human need! How near He is to us, how ready and mighty to help! There are many who remind us of the ship which, after being tossed to and fro by the storm and making no port, was without water, and its crew, fainting with thirst, hailed a passing vessel with the cry, "Water! Water!" to which the reply came back, "Let down your buckets—you are surrounded with fresh water."

They were off the coast of Brazil in the violent rush of the Amazon, which pushes its tide of fresh water away into the Atlantic a hundred miles. O thou thirsty one, thou needst not perish, thou mayest live; as the waters of the deep surround and uphold the floating vessel, so the love of God flows around thy life. Let down the bucket of faith into the ocean of His saving fulness.

There are those who are like Hagar in the wilderness. It is a striking picture. The water in the skin-bottle was spent, the boy was on the point of dying of thirst, and, unable to bear the sight of his sufferings, she laid him under the wild shrubs, and sat down about a bowshot off, in despair. She had no hope for herself nor for her child, until her eyes were opened and the Angel of the Lord showed her a fountain which she had not observed. Let us ask God to open the eyes of our mind, that we may see Him ; for it is quite true

II. That Spiritual Perception leads to Devout and Earnest Supplication.

" Thou wouldest have asked of Him."
There is so much mystery about prayer in its

modes of operation that the wisest may well feel
himself unable to comprehend its workings, and
yet in its main elements it "is the simplest form
of speech that infant lips can try." It is the
language of dependence and desire. Nothing
can be easier than to ask, and the wealth of
Heaven streams into our poor life by prayer.
Many providential gifts are bestowed without
our asking. Think of the long catalogue of
temporal benefits which swell the sum of our
happiness! Fix your mind upon a few of them,
for they are countless in number! How many
of them are answers to prayer? How many of
them are the outcome of our own effort? We
know that He does bless many in their "basket
and store" who do not acknowledge Him at all.
Spiritual blessings, however, are given only to
those who ask. Do you wish to obtain forgive-
ness of sin, regeneration of soul, the Witness of
the Spirit, holiness of life—these are contingent
upon the exercise of fervent and persevering
prayer. "Thus saith the Lord God, I will yet
for this be inquired of by the house of Israel,
to do it for them" (Ezek. xxxvi. 37). When
man was created there was a previous consulta-

tion amongst the Three Persons in the Holy Trinity "Let us make man in our image, after our likeness" (Gen. i. 26); but when man is made a new creature in Christ Jesus, the consultation is between God and man. Divine Sovereignty now moves, not only in obedience to the dictates of infinite mercy, but also in response to the cry of finite weakness. Before He acts, now that He has made such a complete provision for our wants, He waits for some sign of a sense of sin, He listens for the plea of penitent faith. Let it rise from the depths of our consciousness. "Create in me a clean heart, O God, and renew a right spirit within me" (Ps. li. 10). Observe further

III. THAT DEVOUT AND EARNEST SUPPLICA-
TION SECURES THE PROMPT AND GENEROUS
BESTOWAL OF THE BLESSING OF SALVATION.

"He would have given thee living water."

This text is like a house with three apartments, a chain with three links, or a throne with three stepping-stones.

The first is spiritual insight, the second is prayer, and the third is God's love. Of the

three apartments in the palace, this last is the
audience-chamber of the King. Of the three
links in the chain, this last is the strongest and
brightest. Of the three stepping-stones to the
throne, this last is the one that brings us right
up before the Royal Presence. " He would have
given thee living water." Mark the contrast
between His giving and that of the woman.

(*a*) She gave to Him that which could only
quench bodily thirst—water out of a well, which
might run dry at any time and fail in its supply.
He would have given that which would satisfy
the craving of the soul—living water for a living
spirit from a living Fountain.

(*b*) She had to travel a considerable distance
and undergo much inconvenience in fetching
water from Sychar's Well. He would have given
her that secret of a holy and happy experience
which would be, not like a cistern, but a well-
spring within, that would go where she moved
and would remain where she dwelt.

(*c*) She gave Him what He asked in a manner
utterly wanting in grace and courtesy. She was
probably bewildered by the strangeness and
novelty of the situation. If the flow of her

charity was not checked, it is evident that her
mind was influenced to some degree by the re-
membrance of the bitter enmity between the
two nations. Homer says that the gods have
their favourites; but He who came to redeem
all men by His death is no respecter of persons.
He is swayed by no unworthy predilections and
partialities. He asks no question in regard to
nationality. When He gives, it is not with churlish
meagreness or grudging reluctance, but with
gracious readiness and overflowing abundance.

Alexander the Great was not offended when
the indigent philosopher at his court asked for
ten thousand pounds. The Chancellor of the
Imperial Exchequer thought it was a most
presumptuous request. What did Alexander
reply? " Let the money be instantly paid. I
am delighted with the philosopher's way of
thinking. He has done me singular honour : he
treats me like a king ; by the largeness of his
request he shows the idea he has formed of my
wealth and munificence." There is a Monarch
to whom all princes and kings are subjects, in
whose presence Alexander was never great.
The King of Glory is truly and incomparably

5

great,—great in power and great in love,—and
His giving surpasses all.

> " Thou art coming to a King,
> Large petitions with thee bring ;
> For His power and grace are such,
> None can ever ask too much."

Let us cherish lofty views of His goodness, His
generosity, His amazing bounty.

V.

The Preeminence of Christ.

As all waters meet in the sea, and all light in the sun, so all the perfections and excellences of the saints and angels meet in Christ.—DYER.

The Preeminence of Christ.

"Art Thou greater than our father Jacob?"—St. John iv. 12.

SHECHEM or Sychar nestled on the northern slope of Mount Gerizim. At the present time it is called Nablous, a corruption of Neapolis (new city). When the patriarchal pilgrim Abraham went forth on his expedition of faith and obedience, with no geographic map to guide him, and with no idea in his mind as to the route and terminus of his journey, the first place where he pitched a tent and built an altar was under the Oak of Moreh at Shechem. In subsequent ages it became one of the six Cities of Refuge. It was here the Law was re-promulgated, its blessings from Gerizim and its curses from Ebal, and the people bowed their heads

and acknowledged Jehovah to be their King and
Ruler. It was in this picturesque locality that
Joshua, on the eve of his decease, convened the
people and delivered his farewell counsels; and
in the reign of Jeroboam Shechem became for
a time the capital of the kingdom of Israel.
Interesting as these local associations might be
to the general Bible student, in the mind of
the woman of Samaria they were eclipsed by
another event connected with the patriarch
Jacob. Upon his arrival at this city, after a
sojourn in Mesopotamia, Jacob found the Hivites
in possession, with Hamor as their prince, with
whom he negotiated for the purchase of land,
which he bequeathed as a patrimony to his son
Joseph. The property gained additional value
by reason of the well which he had caused to
be dug there. This he did so that he might not
be dependent upon his neighbours for an ample
supply of pure water. We may form some idea
of the superstitious reverence with which the
place was regarded, from the manner in which
it is described by the Evangelist. He does not
state that "the parcel of ground" was near the
city, but that the city was near "the parcel of

ground," which contained the famous well that
had gathered around itself such a halo of
sanctity because of its associations with the
patriarch. She reasoned within herself something after this manner: That if this well was
good enough for their illustrious progenitor, it
was surely good enough for this traveller to
whom she was speaking! " Art Thou greater
than our father Jacob, which gave us the well,
and drank thereof himself, and his children, and
his cattle?" To this question we propose to
give a distinctly affirmative answer. The infinite
glory of Jesus will only appear more resplendent
as the result of comparison with any one, however distinguished. Our design will not be to
unduly disparage the patriarch in order to exalt
the Son of God. There is no need to do this,
and there would be no justification for such a
course of procedure. For every virtue he
possessed, and every worthy exploit he achieved,
we gladly award to Jacob credit and honour;
yet, having placed him as high as it is possible
for us to do, we must confess Jesus to be unspeak-
ably higher,—in fact, He is enthroned in glorious
supremacy.

I. JACOB WAS A PERSON OF HISTORIC NOTE.

He was at the head of a large household, the prince of a tribe of considerable magnitude. He was the owner of much property in cattle and land; he was a little king and priest, occupying a position of immense influence during his lifetime, and, after his decease, his memory had been cherished with increasing reverence and veneration through the ages. With the Jews the great hero was Abraham, the father of the faithful and the friend of God. Their constant boast was, " We have Abraham to our father "; and according to one of their proverbial sayings, he sat near the gates of hell, and suffered no Israelite to go down into it. They thought they were heaping the greatest contumely and contempt on Jesus when they asked the question, " Art Thou greater than our father Abraham ? " (St. John viii. 53). With the Samaritans the favourite patriarch was Jacob. In our Lord's time they were not genuine Israelites, but a corrupted race, sprung from a commingling of heathen nations, who were sent by Esarhaddon, King of Assyria, to Samaria

as colonists. Notwithstanding, however, this
demoralising amalgamation, they claimed the
immunities and privileges peculiar to the Jews.
When Alexander the Great demanded tribute
of them in the Sabbatic year, they asked him
to excuse them because, in harmony with Hebrew
custom, they did not till the land in the seventh
year ; but he pronounced their claim an imposture,
and destroyed their land. At the same time, the
original inhabitants of that province were direct
descendants of Jacob. In the distribution of
Canaan amongst the twelve tribes, it was divided
between the two sons of Joseph, Ephraim and
Manasseh.

The neighbourhood of Sychar was marked
not only by Jacob's Well, but also by Joseph's
Tomb. Both are objects of peculiar interest to
travellers even now ; and there were so many
reminiscences and traditions of the patriarch in
the locality, that it was no wonder the woman
should ask the question, " Art Thou greater than
our father Jacob ? "

Did not God Himself bestow exceptional
honour on him ? Who can forget the scene at
Bethel when the tired fugitive laid down on

the hillside to sleep, with a stone for a pillow; and in his dream saw a mystic Ladder which seemed to rise from the bare ground on which he lay, the top of which reached even unto heaven, and on it angels ascending and descending? He realised that the place was "none other but the house of God, and . . . the gate of heaven" (Gen. xxviii. 17). Who can forget the scene at Peniel when the Angel of the Covenant wrestled with him, and by his importunity Jacob gained so decided a victory that his name was changed to Israel?

The minor prophets refer to him frequently. The Book of Hosea is a pathetic lamentation over the degeneracy of Ephraim as well as Judah; and in it he yearned for their return from their state of alienation, by recalling to their minds the wonders Jehovah wrought for their distinguished ancestor. Malachi cheers the returned exiles by assuring them that the love God had for him was not withheld from his descendants. Altogether, the name of Jacob is one of the most honoured in sacred story. But

II. In Nobility of Character and in Perpetuity of Influence Jesus is Peerless.

It is said that there is something of the angel in the worst of men, and something of the devil in the best. Jacob was not without his virtues and excellences, not without marks of Divine favour,—for Jehovah revealed Himself in early ages as " the God of Jacob,"—but he was not without serious faults and failings.

(*a*) *His life was tarnished with many blemishes —Christ was sinless.*

Jacob was greedy, selfish, and deceitful. He robbed his brother Esau of his birthright and blessing, and imposed upon his dying father. Is such a man worthy to be brought into rivalry with the immaculate Saviour, " who did no sin, neither was guile found in His mouth "? (1 Pet. ii. 22).

Is he fit to be placed in comparison with Him of whom it is said, " Thou art fairer than the children of men : grace is poured into Thy lips : therefore God hath blessed Thee for ever "? (Ps. xlv. 2). Could he have thrown out the bold challenge Christ makes in the 46th verse of the 8th chapter of this Gospel of St. John,

"Which of you convinceth Me of sin"? Such a challenge made to His bitterest enemies can amount to nothing less than a claim to absolute sanctity. Neither foe nor friend could ever discover a flaw in His character, or a rent in his seamless robe. Pilate said, "I find no fault in this man" (Luke xxiii. 4). Pilate's wife said, "Have thou nothing to do with that just man" (Matt. xxvii. 19). Judas declared, "I have sinned in that I have betrayed the innocent blood" (Matt. xxvii. 4); and the dying thief exclaimed, "This man hath done nothing amiss" (Luke xxiii. 41). All the saints that have ever lived, even the holiest of them, have had their imperfections and inconsistencies, and many of them have broken down and failed in the good qualities for which they were famous. Moses was proverbial for his meekness, and yet he disobeyed his Maker; St Peter for his boldness, and yet he denied his Lord; St. John for his love, and yet he asked the Master to command fire from heaven.

How many a spot defiles the robe
That wraps an earthly saint !

Jesus stands alone as stainless Purity embodied in human form.

(b) *Jacob was mortal ; Jesus is the Eternal God.*

Two affirmations were made by our Lord on this subject at this time; and after each statement the Jews, wild with rage, took up stones to cast at Him: materials lying there for the repairing and completion of the Temple were used as missiles to fling at Him who is the Corner-stone of the spiritual temple.

He claims absolute unity with Jehovah. " I and My Father are one " (St. John x. 30). He claims that His life was anterior to that of the founder of the Hebrew nation,—in fact, to be uncreated, and yet existing from and before the beginning.

" Before Abraham was, I am " (St. John viii. 58). Here He appropriates the incommunicable name by which Jehovah revealed Himself to Moses: " I AM " (Ex. iii. 14). This title implies unchangeable essence and everlasting duration. This is the name which the Jews for centuries dared not utter. They saw the word in the reading of the Scriptures, and substituted another in its stead. They regarded it with the greatest reverence. Now our Lord claims it for Himself in its plenitude of sacred meaning. Mark, the statement is not that Christ came into existence before the patriarch, but that He never came into

being at all. "Before Abraham was, I am."
Numerous are the passages which teach or imply
the same truth. As a monarch commissions an
ambassador to represent him in another court, so
God sent His Son nto the world. Thus clearly
affirmed by His own lips, pre-existence is a
substantial and irrefragable proof of His Divinity.

Jacob lived for one hundred and forty-seven
years; but he died, and was gathered to his
fathers. Jesus lives FOR EVER.

(c) Jacob paid his tribute of homage to the
world's Redeemer.

With his dying breath he uttered a memorable prediction respecting the Messiah, and it
was literally fulfilled. "The sceptre shall not
depart from Judah, nor a lawgiver from between
his feet, until Shiloh come, and to Him shall the
gathering of the people be" (Gen. xlix. 10). If
the patriarch had been alive, and had heard this
conversation between our Saviour and the woman
of Samaria, with what indignation would he have
repudiated any idea of equality with, or superiority
to, the Son of God! With what lowly and
genuine adoration would he have bowed down
before Him, and with what eagerness and delight
would he have helped her by Jacob's Well to

behold Jacob's Star and to climb Jacob's Ladder! These great old saints of other days counted it their highest honour to be heralds of the King, and foretellers of His glory. They had prophetic glimpses of Him who would redeem humanity by His life and death, and through the dusk of centuries they saw afar off the Lamb of God on the altar of Calvary. Their hearts and hopes turned to Him as the rivers to the sea; as the needle to the pole; as the flowers and plants to the sun. In company with "the goodly fellowship of the prophets," Jacob bore his witness and brought his tribute.

The science of comparative theology makes us familiar with the sages of heathendom, and the founders of various religions or codes of ethics prevailing in different countries. Augustine says that "there is no religion that does not contain some grains of truth." Read the story of these heroes of paganism, Sakya-muni, Mahomet, Zoroaster, and Confucius; study their life and character; note their influence over their votaries. We acknowledge that they towered above their fellows, as huge mountains rise above neighbouring hills; but between them and the Son of God there is a distance as great as that between the highest peak of the Alps or the Himalayas and the third heaven—a distance which is immeasurable. " To whom, then, will ye liken Me, or shall I be equal, saith the Holy One?" (Isa. xl. 25). Has He any peer among patriarchs, prophets, apostles, martyrs, confessors? He is greater than the greatest.

Renan says, "Whatever may be the unlooked-for phenomena of the future, Jesus will not be surpassed." As far as ancient heroes are concerned, it is generally admitted that He is transcendently above all comparison ; and a sceptic now declares that He will have the undisputed supremacy of the future. Renan's confession reminds us of the magnificent utterance of the apostle, so vast in the sweep of its significance: " Wherefore God hath highly exalted Him, and given Him a name which is above every other name. That at the name of Jesus every knee should bow, of things in heaven, and things in earth, and things under the earth. And that every tongue should confess that Jesus Christ is Lord, to the glory of God the Father " (Phil. ii. 9-11).

Will you bow before Him in adoration and praise? Will you accept His mercy and own His authority?

VI.

Spiritual Worship.

Even to the chosen three Christ imparted no truth more profound than these. He admits this poor schismatic to the fountain-head of religion.—DR. PLUMMER.

Worship that is false will kill the soul as quickly as no worship.

Spiritual Worship.

"Our fathers worshipped in this mountain ; and ye say, that in Jerusalem is the place where men ought to worship. . . But the hour cometh, and now is, when the true worshippers shall worship the Father in spirit and in truth ; for the Father seeketh such to worship Him."—St. John iv. 20-23.

I T is a striking fact that the woman of Samaria did not realise the Divinity of the Stranger with whom she conversed until the lamp of Omniscience threw its searchlight on the dark recesses of her life. The awakening of her moral consciousness was coincident with the manifestation of His Deity in the knowledge He showed of the secrets of her history.

Christ might have selected some other mode of impressing her with the idea of His superhuman authority. In Judea, whence He had just come,

He performed many miracles, and, notwithstanding temporary enthusiasm, the general treatment He received was cold and contemptuous. In Samaria His ministry was marked by no startling demonstrations of His power over the laws of nature; and yet the welcome was warm and cordial. In Judea His miracles were deeds; in Samaria they were words instinct with spirit and life. No sooner had He spoken of the culpable complications of the woman's social relationships than she made two discoveries: (1) That this Stranger was no ordinary Jew, but the Messiah. He possessed the attribute of Omniscience. (2) That the same flash of celestial illumination which revealed His Divinity, revealed to her also the enormity of her transgression. She felt the pungency of what He said. But as a bird that has been shot, yet not killed, covers the wound under its feathers, and tries to soar as if nothing had happened: in like manner, although painfully conscious of the truth of the charge, with remarkable skill and affected indifference, she diverts the course of the conversation from this unpalatable subject to the long-standing controversy between the Jew and the Samaritan respecting the rival claims of the two temples, that on Mount Zion, and the other on Mount Gerizim. Christ declines to be drawn into the meshes of this old dispute, pronounces no verdict in favour of either side, and makes use of the digression made by her in order to deliver words of wondrous sublimity on the nature and scope of worship. Observe—

I. IT IS AN INTERNAL ATTITUDE, NOT AN EXTERNAL FORM.

" In spirit and in truth " (ver. 23).

It has been remarked that there are many countries without art, science, literature, and philosophy, but none without prayer. The existence of idolatry confirms the universal prevalence of the instinct of worship. Man is a worshipping animal. Of all the creatures God has made, he is the only one who can render intelligent homage to his Maker. The nature of the homage is determined by the character of the object worshipped. As there is infinite disparity between an idol and the God of Heaven (1 Cor. viii. 4), so there is measureless contrast between the gross, sensuous, and debasing idolatry of the heathen

and the spiritual and ennobling worship of the
Christian. One of the main features of the
religion of the Bible is, that it enjoins the duty of
adoration to a Being who is invisible to the eye
of the body. Augustine tells us of a pagan who
showed him his idols, saying, " Here are my gods ;
where is thine? " Augustine says, " I showed him
not my God, not because I had not One to show
him, but because he had not eyes to see Him."

His works are visible everywhere: in the
beauties of nature, in the glories of the Bible, in
the wonders of Providence; but He is invisible
except to the eye of faith.

The Holy Book supplies us with a fuller knowledge of Him than any other medium except the
Incarnate Word; and the author of the Fourth
Gospel tells us more about His essence and nature
than any other inspired writer. In the Epistles
he says, " God is Light " (1 St. John i. 5), and
" God is Love " (1 St. John iv. 8). In the Gospel
he says, " God is a Spirit " (St. John iv. 24).
Presumably the Evangelist, in these three phrases,
simply quotes words which fell from the lips of
Him who is the eternal Son of God, during
seasons of rapt and exalted communion. Do we

find in them any hints and intimations of the
doctrine of the Trinity of personal subsistences
in the unity of the Godhead?

"God is Love": the Father whose tender compassion is the primary source of our redemption.

"God is Light": the Son who is the Light
of the world, whose mission it was to execute the
loving designs of the Father, and to illumine
our darkness by coming as the Day-spring from
on high.

"God is a Spirit": the Holy Ghost, proceed-
ing from the Father and the Son, the Author
and Giver of life. In the representations of
Scripture the Unity of the Divine Essence is quite
as conspicuous as the Trinity of persons. The
works of Creation, Preservation, Redemption, are
ascribed to all interchangeably, and to no one
exclusively. The designation which we take in
general to be applicable more directly to the Third
Person is here employed in regard to the essential
Unity of the Godhead, to the Three in One and
the One in Three: Father, Son, and Holy Ghost.

"God is a Spirit."

All the objects that exist may be divided into
two classes. There are those which are material,

palpable, capable of being felt yet having no
feeling. There are those which are spiritual,
intelligent, sentient. Matter cannot think and
feel; mind can do both. Where there are the
capacities of affection, volition, judgment, there is
a spirit, whether in man or in God: with this
difference, that in the former it is finite, in the
latter it is infinite. Who can define a spirit?
It is easy to say what it is not, impossible to state
exactly what it is. We can tell any substance by
its form and colour, or we can feel its weight.
Matter we know; but of a spirit we are ready to
ask, Who art thou? What art thou? By One who
knew all about the subject we are told that "a
spirit hath not flesh and bones." He could have
given us, if He had thought it wise, a more definite
and positive definition. But with the help of the
clearest explanations we should still be unable to
rise to the altitude of the theme. "Canst thou by
searching find out God? Canst thou find out the
Almighty unto perfection?" (Job xi. 7).

(a) If He be a Spirit it follows, as a natural
sequence, that our homage is to be "in spirit."
This sounds the death - knell of the gross
superstitions of Paganism, and the elaborate

ceremonial of Judaism. An idol might be
served with bended knees and uplifted hands
only. He who is a Spirit accepts only the adoration of the heart, the intellect, and the conscience.
Worship does not lie in sacrifices and oblations,
but " in spirit." In China, according to Medhurst,
the priests of Buddha understand and teach the
doctrine of the assimilation of the worshipper to
the object worshipped. They say: "Think of
Buddha and you will be transformed to Buddha.
If men pray to Buddha, and do not become
Buddha, it is because the mouth prays, and not
the mind." With equal propriety may we not
say : " Think of God and you will be transformed
to His likeness. If men pray to Him and do not
become like Him, it is because the mouth prays,
and not the heart "?

Jesus says nothing here about forms in religious
service. This was not because they were not
necessary in a rational degree as expressions of
the inner life, but because they received exagger-
ated prominence from the religionists of His time.
History repeats itself. Pharisees of old have their
representatives to-day in those who lay too much
stress upon externalisms : who " tithe mint and

rue, and every herb, and pass over judgment and
the love of God" (Luke xi. 42, R.V.).

(*b*) Christian worship is to be offered "in
truth." The word "truth" has two distinct mean-
ings in the New Testament. Sometimes it stands
in opposition to the figurative or typical, as the
substance to the shadow; at other times, in con-
tradistinction to the false, deceitful, and treacher-
ous. Here it embodies the two significations.
The sacrifice of the ancient Jew is a prophetic
adumbration of the atonement of Calvary, and
it finds its antitypical fulfilment in the blessed
reality of personal consecration on the part of the
Christian believer. He gives to God, and lays on
the altar neither lamb, goat, dove, nor pigeon, but
himself. Dr. Martineau says, that to give Him
something we have is heathen, to give Him something we do is Jewish, and to give what we are
is Christian. We are to present ourselves unto
God. Nothing is more beautiful than truth, and
this He requires in our whole life; and specially
is the worship which we present to Him to
bear the stamp of sincerity and consistency. Let
there be correspondence between the outer form
and the inner life. Shall we pray to be heard of

men? Shall we give to be seen of men? Shall we fast to be admired for our self-denial? Whatever we do, let us be true and genuine in our approach to Him who "searcheth all hearts and understandeth all the imaginations of the thoughts." Jesus teaches, respecting worship, that

II. IT IS FILIAL DEVOTION, NOT SLAVISH DREAD.

"For the Father seeketh such to worship Him." (ver. 23).

There is only one reference here to God as a Spirit, whereas there are three allusions to Him as a Father. His Fatherhood presupposes His Spirituality, and much more that is delightful and attractive. God is a Spirit: as such He is invisible and incomprehensible, and Herbert Spencer is justified in regarding Him as " unknowable." God is a Father: that is a revelation which is luminous with love and endearing in its tenderness. Well might Philip ask,—and the petition embodies a deep and universal longing of the human heart,—" Lord shew us the Father, and it sufficeth us " (St. John xiv. 8). No representation of God could be more beautiful or better

calculated to inspire confidence in us toward Him.
As Lawgiver, Judge, Sovereign, He should receive
our obedience, submission, and allegiance; as
Father He calls forth our gratitude, trust, and
love. Dr. David Thomas says, that as the genial
sun of May stirs the choristers of the grove into
music, the presence of the Father will not only
hush all the cries of the child, but fill the heart
with filial rapture.

Paternity implies the communication of two
elements — life and likeness. There may be
likeness without life. A painter produces a
picture, or a sculptor carves a statue of himself—
in a sense he is the father of it. There is likeness, but no life.

On the other hand, there may be life and no
likeness. In the light of Creation, Providence,
and Redemption, the blackest criminal may
endorse Paul's quotation from classic poetry, "We
are also His offspring" (Acts xvii. 28). The
Pharisees had life, but no likeness. In their spirit
and actions they bore a stronger resemblance to
the great adversary of God and men. "Ye are of
your father the devil, and the lusts of your father
ye will do. He was a murderer from the begin-

ning. . . . He is a liar, and the father of it" (St
John viii. 44).

If a man disgraces himself and his family by
the commission of flagrant crime, or by under-
going imprisonment or the full penalty of the
law on the gallows, his child will be ashamed
of his relationship to him. The Pharisees could
not be proud of their parentage. Those who
are the children of God glory in Him as their
Father: they adore His infinite perfections,
and rejoice in His wisdom, power, holiness,
and love. Where there is real spiritual life, there
will be likeness. If we are "born, not of blood,
nor of the will of the flesh, nor of the will of man,
but of God" (St. John i. 13), we shall bear His
image. If we are partakers of the Divine nature
we shall resemble our Heavenly Father, and we
shall approach Him in prayer, not with servile
terror, but with childlike trust. A few years ago
an Indian Brahmin became a Christian. By the
operation of an unjust law he was deprived of
his property, separated from his family, and cast
on the world in abject poverty. Loathed as
a leper by his dearest relatives, the question
was put to him, "What have you gained by

becoming a Christian?" "Much," he replied.
"Much—I have learned to say, 'Our Father
which art in heaven.'" Further, respecting worship,
Christ teaches that

III. IT IS UNIVERSAL: NOT LIMITED BY LOCAL RESTRICTIONS.

"Our fathers worshipped in this mountain," etc.
(verses 20, 21, 23).

One cannot help being struck with the tone
of profound veneration with which the woman
referred to Gerizim, which to her and her co-
religionists was the holy mountain of the world.
It was alleged in Samaritan legends that on its
summit was the seat of Paradise, and from its
dust Adam was formed, the spot being pointed
out where he erected his first altar; that it was
the Ararat on which the ark rested, which the
waters of the Deluge never overflowed, and no
dead thing, borne by the Flood, had defiled; that
the exact locality could be identified where Noah
reared an altar after the waters had subsided, and
the seven steps, on each of which he offered
sacrifice; that the altar was standing on which
Abraham bound his son Isaac, and the place

pointed out where the ram was caught; that on its summit is Bethel, where Jacob dreamt of the ladder, and vowed a vow; and that there Moses buried the Tabernacle, with its vessels. Of course the Jews laughed at these wild assertions, and treated them as examples of astounding credulity. Even to-day the miserable remnant of the Samaritan nation cling to their sacred mountain with passionate and indestructible devotion. We do not know whether the woman of Samaria accepted for facts these traditional myths. Probably she did, for she cherished the deepest reverence for the place, and specially for the temple on its brow. " Our fathers worshipped in this mountain." Schiller says that " time consecrates, and what is grey with age becomes religion "; and Henry Ward Beecher tells us that " opinions, like electricity, are supposed to descend more safely along an unbroken chain." The mind of this woman was imbued with intense attachment to ancestral custom and association. She was probably a direct descendant of those Ephraimites who could not pronounce the *sh* in Shibboleth. Proverbial is the force of habit, and potent is the influence of custom and tradition

even in our religious life. We are swayed by
them to a greater extent than we are disposed to
acknowledge. We are attached, naturally enough,
to certain places of worship, because they are
hallowed by inspiring memories. They were
scenes of heavenly blessing to our parents and
progenitors, and to us, their descendants, they are
endeared by the recollection of personal help and
inspiration received from God within their walls.
It is perfectly legitimate and commendable to
admire what is ancient and venerable in religion,
as in art or architecture. Let us not forget,
however, that the ultimate basis of authority is
not antiquity, but efficacy. The question is not,
Which is the oldest? but, Which is the best?
though it does not follow, of necessity, that we
must cast aside the thoughts and actions of our
fathers as useless or injurious. Let us honour
their names and memories with the greatest
loyalty possible. At the same time, let us bear
in mind that we live in a day when the light of
Heaven shines with brighter lustre, and that we
require for ourselves a fresh, vital, and personal
realisation of the presence of God. Do not
imagine that He is limited to your Gerizim. His

love is larger than any Church and wider than any creed. Christ gives a new idea of worship, in which it stands emancipated from the fetters forged and the boundary walls erected by bigotry. He enlarges its area so as to make it coextensive with the universe. It is not at Gerizim nor yet at Jerusalem, but anywhere and everywhere wherever earnest believers are gathered together. Where there are devout souls engaged in prayer and praise, that spot becomes as sacred as any temple. This idea was new and yet old, for saintly spirits in all ages have felt its truth and blessedness. Jacob's Bethel was in the open air, with a stone for his pillow and a sky for a canopy. Hezekiah's oratory was a room in a house. David prayed in the wild desert; Daniel in the lions' den; Shadrach, Meshach, and Abednego in the furnace of fire; Christ on the mountain and in the garden; Peter on the housetop; Paul and Silas in prison; and John on the island of Patmos.

In course of time most systems of religion show a strong and decided tendency towards centralisation: Judaism at Jerusalem, Samaritanism at Gerizim, Mahometanism at Mecca, Confucianism at Pekin, and Popery at Rome.

Christ counteracts this tendency by emphasising,
not the externalisms of religious service, but the
paramount importance of spirituality of mind,
purity of motive, and singleness of aim. Do
not say that "Christ is here" or "Christ is there,"
for He is everywhere.

O Thou to whom in ancient time
The lyre of Hebrew bards was strung,
Whom kings adored in song sublime,
And prophets praised with glowing tongue.
Not now on Zion's height alone
The favoured worshipper may dwell,
Nor where, at sultry noon, Thy Son
Sat weary by the patriarch's well.
From every place below the skies
The grateful song, the fervent prayer,
The incense of the heart, may rise
To Heaven, and find acceptance there.

VII.

A Great Change.

Not many wise, rich, noble, or profound
In science, win one inch of heavenly
ground.—COWPER.

His birth had been first revealed by night to
a few unknown and ignorant shepherds : the
first full clear announcement by Himself of His
own Messiahship was made by a well-side in the
weary noon to a single obscure Samaritan
woman. And to this poor, sinful, ignorant
stranger had been uttered words of immortal
significance, to which all future ages would
listen, as it were, with hushed breath and on
their knees.—DEAN FARRAR.

VII.

𝔄 𝔊reat 𝔠hange.

" The woman saith unto Him, I know that Messias cometh, which is called Christ: when He is come, He will tell us all things."—St. John iv. 25.

" Jesus saith unto her, I that speak unto thee am He."— St. John iv. 26.

" The woman . . . . saith to the men, Come, see a man which told me all things that ever I did: is not this the Christ ? "—St. John iv. 28-29.

PONTIUS, the biographer of St. Cyprian, passes by the early period of his history entirely with the remark that a man's actions should be recorded, not from the time of his first but second birth. The new life dates its origin from the moment of conversion. The old man with his lusts is crucified, and his corpse is buried in the grave, and no one wishes for a resurrection ; no one cares to read his memoir or hear a recital

101

of his impious exploits in the time prior to his regeneration. These doings in which he once revelled are now gladly allowed to sink into oblivion; they serve only as reminders of the completeness of the transformation, as a milestone marks the distance the pilgrim has travelled on his journey. With inimitable skill Bunyan describes the progress of a believer from the City of Destruction to the New Jerusalem. Our interest in the allegory is excited at once by reading how he passed through the wicket-gate into the road that leads to the Celestial City, over whose portal is the inscription, "Knock, and it shall be opened unto you." More than once the Apostle Paul narrated the story of his conversion; and the Evangelist John renders noble service by his graphic reproduction of the facts associated with the great crisis in the spiritual history of the woman of Samaria, when she was led out of the darkness of unbelief into the light of intelligent faith. In its initial stage the change in her was sudden, and in its subsequent development it was gradual. In speaking of and to Jesus she employs various titles, and these mark so many steps in the gradation of spiritual enlightenment: "Jew" (ver. 9), "Sir" (ver. 15), "Prophet" (ver. 19). There were three periods in her experience, which may be described by three words: Expectation, Revelation, Commendation.

I. EXPECTATION.

"I know that Messias cometh, which is called Christ: when He is come, He will tell us all things" (ver. 25).

Ignorant as she was at that moment when she uttered these words in regard to the personal claims of Jesus, she displays acquaintance with two subjects, both of which are intimately related to each other: (*a*) that the Messias was expected; and (*b*) that He would be distinguished by the possession of the attribute of Omniscience. Among the Jews there was a general feeling of hope, based upon the predictions of ancient prophecy. These prognostications were not vague and indefinite, but minute and exact, even to the place where, and the time when, He would be born, the manner of His appearance, the object of His mission, the variety and cruelty of His sufferings, and the glory and perpetuity of His triumphs. Among the Gentiles there was a longing for a Deliverer, and even a settled conviction that One would appear. The existence of this expectation is confirmed by the testimony of classical writers such as Suetonius and Tacitus, and by the conduct of the Magi, who were looking out for the star, and who, when it appeared in the sky, followed its guidance to the manger in which lay the Holy Child. As the Samaritans were an amalgam of Jews and Gentiles, it is not strange to find that they shared in this hope: they accepted the Pentateuch, and those sacred documents foretold the advent of the Messiah (Deut. xviii. 15). The Jews were expecting Him as a king with temporal sovereignty; the Samaritans as a prophet with supernatural wisdom.

About a hundred years after the Incarnation there sprang up a notorious impostor, who headed an insurrection against the Romans under the Emperor Hadrian. He fought at first with great success against the Romans, and even compelled them to evacuate Jerusalem, where he was proclaimed king, and caused coins to be struck with his superscription. His name was Simon, but he called himself Barcochba, *i.e.* son of the star, pretending that the prediction should be fulfilled in him, " There shall come a Star out of Jacob" (Num. xxiv. 17).

After having been deceived by him for two years, his contemporaries decided at last to apply this test: they brought before him a number of persons whom he did not know; they desired him to point out those who were the righteous, and those who were the vicious. He failed miserably, and they put him to death. Christ the true Messiah fulfilled in Himself the hope of the nations as expressed in the words of the woman. If He did not literally tell her all things, He told her quite enough for her to be convinced that He was the Omniscient Son of God. But, after all, it was no mere guesswork on her part: it was a

II. REVELATION.

" I that speak unto thee am He" (ver. 26).

It was not long after she began to think and speak of Him, when He made Himself known to her. It was while the two disciples were on their way to Emmaus, rapt in eager thought and

conversation about the Risen One that He over-
took them on their journey, and opened unto
them the Scriptures, so that they recognised in
their Companion their Divine Lord and Master.
If you desire Him to favour you with an
Epiphany or an Apocalypse, think of Him not
with cold unbelief, but with ardent longing.

It is a significant fact that our Lord never
spoke in such explicit terms concerning Himself
to His own countrymen, nor to His disciples,
till a short time before His death. Not even to
John the Baptist did he say, " I am He."

It is supposed that the woman was thus
honoured because she was alone, and a
Samaritan. In making the declaration thus
privately, and to one who belonged to another
nation, it is thought that He would have no
reason to apprehend that His ministry would be
terminated before His hour had arrived. We
are inclined to believe that the reason why the
disclosure was made to this woman, and withheld
from the Pharisees, was because she manifested
a spirit of which they were destitute—a spirit
which was receptive and docile. He had nothing
but rebuke for the arrogant and self-complacent;

nothing but healing for the broken in heart. He reserved the choicest unveilings of Himself for the humble and the meek. Religion makes its appeal to the moral rather than to the intellectual faculties, *i.e.* to the love of truth, the desire for goodness, the sense of need ; not to ability or learning (St. Matt. xi. 25). Once let the inner citadel of the affections be captured, and before long the outer works of the fortress are His. Let the heart yield its love, and soon the intellect will pay its mark of fealty. The disciples marvelled that He talked with the woman, yet no man said, " *Why* talkest Thou with her ? " They would have found that the answer, if He had deigned to give it, contained the reason of His procedure, *i.e.* that He found her nature to be fit and suitable soil in which to plant the seed of heavenly truth. Carlyle says that women are born worshippers. Crabbe sings—

> Woman sees deep, man sees far :
> To the man, the world is his heart ;
> To the woman, the heart is her world.

Although sin stained the life of this woman, it had not destroyed wholly her spiritual sensibilities. There is a reflex influence, as a rule, between tutor and pupil: the tutor, by his skill and tact in the art of teaching, inspires the pupil; the pupil, by quickness of perception and aptness in learning, inspires the tutor. There is the same electric current at work between the preacher and the hearer: the preacher acts on the hearer by the lofty enthusiasm of his spirit, the impressiveness of his manner, and his absorption in his theme; the hearer reacts on the preacher by the interest and sympathy with which he listens. There is a connection between devoutness in the pew and power in the pulpit.

Did our fathers preach better than we do? If they did, it may be because they had better hearers, whose minds were less preoccupied with the affairs of this life, and more eager to receive the message of the Gospel. Good hearers often create good preachers.

Jesus touched the memory and the conscience of this woman. She felt herself to be a sinner; she became a penitent believer, a most responsive and appreciative auditor: hence He revealed Himself to her as the Messiah, and discoursed to her on some of the most fundamental and sublime verities of the Christian faith.

The third stage in her spiritual progress may be represented by the word

III. COMMENDATION.

" The woman . . . . saith to the men, Come, see a man which told me all things that ever I did : is not this the Christ ? " (verses 28, 29).

When the philosopher of Syracuse, Archimedes, discovered how to test the purity of the gold in the crown of Hiero, and the idea first flashed across his mind, in a transport of joy he ran home to try the experiment, shouting, " Eureka ! Eureka ! " When the woman of Samaria found out with whom she was conversing, in her ecstasy of delight she left her waterpot by the well, and rushed into the city of Sychar to publish the discovery. She was brave, for she went amongst the neighbours who knew her life of sin ; and, moreover, she was highly successful in her mission, for " many of the Samaritans believed on Him because of the word of the woman " (ver. 39, R.V.).

The great naturalist, Huber, tells us that if a wasp discovers a deposit of honey, it will return to its nest and impart the tidings to its companions, who will sally forth in great numbers to share in the sumptuous repast.

In the Gospel of Jesus Christ there is provision sweeter than honey and more precious than gold. Shall we enjoy the banquet in selfish isolation? Can we be silent and not tell others? Shall we not invite them to the feast? Do we realise the meaning and feel the force of the hymn we some- times sing?

> The mercy I feel, to others I show :
> I set to my seal that Jesus is true ;
> Ye all may find favour who come at His call :
> Oh, come to my Saviour, His grace is for all.
>
> Oh, let me commend my Saviour to you :
> The publican's Friend, and Advocate too ;
> For you He is pleading His merits and death
> With God interceding for sinners beneath."

This woman did the work of a home missionary in a spirit which had a beautiful blend of zeal and modesty. She relates simply what has occurred, and draws a legitimate inference. "Is not this the Christ?" In the absence of any dogmatic statement, there is no vagueness of belief or uncertainty of conviction. She is definite and decided, but not dictatorial, in the expression of her new views and feelings: she shows great tact in putting the matter in this form, and in not wishing them to accept her testimony without personal inquiry. She is not trammelled in her movements by any considerations of ecclesiastical etiquette. No Paul had as yet arisen and penned those memorable words to the Corinthian Christians: "Let the women keep silence in the churches" (1 Cor. xiv. 34, R.V.). As yet there were no ecclesiastical organisations in existence. She was acting under the influence of a Heaven-inspired impulse; she was fulfilling the prediction of Joel, "Your sons and your daughters shall prophesy" (Joel ii. 28). She was unconsciously following in the wake of such godly women as Deborah, Hannah, Hulda, and Anna.

The new version of the Bible has given us a rendering of Psalm lxviii. 11 which is entirely different from the Authorised Version: "The Lord giveth the word. The *women* that publish the tidings are a great host."

On the occasion of any signal victory it was customary for the women to gather together and express their gratitude for deliverance with music and dancing. When the Israelites escaped the perils of the Red Sea, and were safely landed on the other side, Miriam, the prophetess, took a timbrel in her hand, and all the women went out after her with timbrels, and they sang, " Sing ye to the Lord, for He hath triumphed gloriously. The horse and the rider hath He thrown into the sea " (Ex. xv. 20, 21). Jephthah's daughters formed a choir of virgins, and with music and dances came out to meet their father, to celebrate his conquest (Judg. xi. 34). After David's successful combat with the giant Goliath, the maidens came out of the cities of Israel to meet King Saul with instruments of music, and formed themselves into two sections, singing antiphonally, " Saul hath slain his thousands, and David his ten thousands (1 Sam. xviii. 6, 7).

Women are engaged to-day, in increasing numbers, in the service of God. They may be seen toiling amid the grime and the crime of the slums in our populous towns and cities, and doing valiant work amid the difficulties and discouragements of foreign countries. " The Lord gave the word ; the women that publish the tidings are a great host."

With respect to the question of sexes, it is vain
to preach the doctrine of equality. With his sterner
physique, man should bear the heavier burden and
do the rougher task. With her tact and tenderness, woman, however, may succeed where man
may fail. She can do effective and noble work
for Him in various spheres of holy activity. Some
time since, in one of our large towns, a man who
was devoid of the fear of God lay on his dying
bed. Several men, anxious lest he should go into
eternity unprepared to meet his Maker and Judge,
called at the house, but he declined to see any of
them. One day a refined and devoted lady was
at the door, and by her winning way found no
difficulty in gaining entrance to the house, and
into the room where the man lay on the verge of
death. She made good use of her opportunity :
she did not shrink from speaking of those things
which appertain to God and Heaven and Christ.
After this, the man was grateful for a visit from
anyone, whether minister or leader, and passed
away from earth with a sure hope of everlasting
life. Home may be woman's chief, but certainly
not her only, sphere of service. Can she not
teach in the Sunday school ? conduct a class for

spiritual fellowship or biblical instruction ; or, with her stores of sympathy, be a messenger of comfort in the sick-room ? Whatever gift she has, let it be used for God and the common good. If her heart be charged with love to Jesus Christ, she will employ her talent, and discover new methods of leading others to Him. The question of " Woman's Rights " has a spiritual aspect. She has—

> The right to shed new joy on earth,
> The right to feel the soul's high worth,
> The right to lead the soul to God,
> Along the path her Saviour trod.

VIII.

The Model Worker.

We take not our meat by duty . . . when service comes to the sentiment of duty, it is near to its dissolution.—EDWARD IRVING.

He most lives who thinks most, feels the noblest, acts the best.—BAILEY.

Live greatly : so shalt thou acquire
Unknown capacities of joy.
                    COVENTRY PATMORE.

Cﬁe (Mo₯ef ᵂorﬁer.

'My meat is to do the will of Him that sent me, and to nish His work."—St. John, iv. 34.

B EFORE the intercourse between Jesus and the Samaritan woman closed, He underwent a process of transformation. Tired with the journey, He rested His wearied frame, and sent His disciples into the city for food. When they returned, they found Him wondrously changed. They could understand why He was no longer tired, for He had reposed by the well. They could understand why He was no longer thirsty, for the woman had given Him a refreshing draught of water. They could not understand, however, why He was no longer hungry, when no man had given Him ought to eat. To them, this was a painful mystery. In the interval of

their absence, striking events had occurred, of
which they had only an imperfect knowledge.
At the well He had met a woman who had
engaged His attention, and stirred His sympathy,
and elicited from His lips words of Divine im-
port. Impressed with what she heard, she
became a fervid evangelist to the inhabitants of
Sychar, who, roused by her invitation, now come
in crowds. No doubt the rest and the cooling
draught refreshed Him, and tended to banish
every symptom of languor ; but these do not
account for His marvellous buoyancy. It
was the thought of the great awakening that
had already commenced amongst the people
which lifted Him above the sensation of hunger.
His disciples were alarmed, and said, " Master,
eat." What does He say? " I have meat to eat
that ye know not of" (ver. 32). As Peter's hearers
on the Day of Pentecost regarded the excitement
under whose influence he acted as spirituous, and
not spiritual, so the disciples even could not
now appreciate the holy exultation which raised
Jesus above the desire for food. Their perplexity
deepened until He gave the reason of His
abstinence from food in this verse, which recalls

the answer He gave to Satan in the desert, when tempted after prolonged fasting to exercise His Omnipotence in turning stones into bread: " Man shall not live by bread alone, but by every word that proceedeth out of the mouth of God " (Matt. iv. 4).

We learn here

I. THAT ONE OF THE DOMINANT FEATURES OF THE IDEAL LIFE WAS SERVICE.

" To *do* the will of Him that sent Me, and to finish His *work*."

Christ was the Ideal Man, and His was the Ideal life. Times for communion He had with the Father, but the trend of His habits was not in the line of philosophic abstraction nor ascetic seclusion, but beneficent activity. As a rule, the Orientalist seeks the minimum of work with the maximum of repose. The heat of the climate is decidedly unfavourable to strenuous exertion. Hence the flowing robe and loose slippers generally worn in Eastern countries. With our Saviour it was otherwise. He performed the maximum of work with the minimum of rest. The scene of His earliest associations was the carpenter's shop, where, under the super-vision of Joseph, He learnt the use of the chisel, the saw, the plane, and to make articles of furniture and implements of agriculture. He conferred dignity by His example on manual toil. When He entered upon the duties of His public ministry, He resisted every temptation to ease and indolence, always acting under a solemn sense of obligation. He said: "We must work the works of Him that sent Me, while it is day: the night cometh, when no man can work" (St. John ix. 4, R.V.). "I am in the midst of you as He that serveth" (St. Luke xxii. 27, R.V.). "The Son of man came not to be ministered unto, but to minister, and to give His life a ransom for many" (St. Matt. xx. 28). He was no dreamy theorist, no recluse, no hermit. He lived in noble and self-denying deeds: not in mere thoughts, which are the seed, nor in mere words, which are the blossoms, but in deeds, which are the ripe and precious fruit. We do not disparage the germs: let them grow. We do not depreciate the blossoms: let them flourish; but the tree does not reach its glory and ultimate development until the rich clusters of

fruit hang from its branches. His thoughts and
words matured into acts of loving and unselfish
piety. Dr. Martineau says: "It was not by
retiring into Himself, but by going out of
Himself, that Christ overcame the world; not
by spiritual pathology and self-torture, but by
veritable sufferings, that He became perfect; not
by measuring his own emotions, but by an
oblivion of them in a crowd of toils, a succession
of fulfilled resolves, a profuse expenditure of life
and effort, having others, for their object that He
rose above the dignity of men, and ripened the
divinest spirit for the skies." The creed of
this eminent theologian differs materially from
ours, yet these eloquent words of his remind
us of the eulogy pronounced on the Master
by the Apostle Peter: "Who went about doing
good" (Acts x. 38). No one among the
apostles was better acquainted with the private
and public activities of His life; no one saw
more of His miracles, and no one heard more
of His discourses. In every respect he was
qualified to express an opinion on such a subject;
and this he did in a phrase which, as an epigram
or an aphorism, is not unworthy of the inspired

fisherman, and, as a truth, is a faithful mirror of Him who was Heaven's Ambassador and earth's best Benefactor.

> And so the Word had breath and wrought
> With human hands, the creed of creeds.
> In loveliness of perfect deeds,
> More strong than all poetic thought.

II. THAT THIS SERVICE WAS REGULATED BY CONFORMITY TO A DIVINE CANON.

" The will of Him that sent Me."

In our conduct we are influenced frequently by caprice, impulse, and selfishness. We think ourselves at liberty to do that which is in accordance with our natural inclination. How wide is the gulf between our life and His, who was always moved by the spirit of unswerving loyalty and active obedience to His Father's will! His Incarnation was the embodiment of a beautiful and perfect ideal in the mind of God. The builder erects the structure according to the designs of the architect. All the arrangements of the Tabernacle were made after a pattern exhibited beforehand to Moses.

" The Word was made flesh, and dwelt among

us" (St. John i. 14). Literally, the word "dwelt" means "tabernacled." As the sacred tent of worship where the Shekinah shone was in the centre of the Hebrew encampment, so "He dwelt among us, and we beheld His glory." This Tabernacle was built in harmony with the model in the Eternal mind. It would be irreverent to speculate as to when or where the human Christ realised the Divine purpose in regard to Himself. The Jewish lawgiver was shown the pattern of the holy tent when he was on the mount. We have many pictures of Jesus on the height of these lofty physical eminences. He preached His great sermon on a mount. He was transfigured on a mount. He ascended to Heaven from a mount. We know not, however, when the pattern was exhibited to Him. It may be that there was no need for any disclosure to be made. Before His appearance in human form, He was familiar with it by virtue of His Divinity. But we, like Moses, need the revelation ; and most lives, even the most monotonous, have their peaks of spiritual eleva-tion. Ascending from the plain of humdrum duty to the summit of these serene heights, we are favoured with a vision of God and a glimpse of the ideal life ; we have opened before our mind's eye what we may become. God shows to us at such times the pattern according to which our lives are to be moulded : it is not a question of gratifying self and sense, but of obeying Him. His word is law, His will is the canon of duty. He who gives to us the vision and the inspiration will help us to carry out our resolves into practice, to fulfil our destiny, to realise the longings and the possibilities of our immortal nature. He will not leave nor forsake us when we are compelled to descend from the mount of privilege to the valley of ordinary life.

> We cannot kindle when we will
> The fire which in the heart resides :
> The spirit bloweth and is still,
> In mystery our soul abides ;
> But tasks in hours of insight will'd
> Can be through hours of gloom fulfill'd.

III. THAT THIS SERVICE WAS NOT IRKSOME, BUT PLEASANT AND ALL-ABSORBING.

"My meat is to do the will of Him that sent Me," etc.

In the fortieth Psalm words are used which could not apply to David, and refer to no other than the Son of God, in whom they receive a fitting and exquisite fulfilment: "Lo, I am come; in the roll of the book it is written of Me: I delight to do Thy will, O My God; yea, Thy law is within My heart" (Ps. xl. 7, 8, R.V.). In the previous verse He is represented as saying, "Mine ears hast Thou opened," or, as it is in the margin, "digged or pierced." The boring of the ear was a sign that the enslavement was not only perpetual, but voluntary. The King of kings and Lord of lords became a slave willingly, and He found the service to be no degrading bondage, no galling drudgery. "I delight to do Thy will, O My God." He had ineffable joy in executing the commission with which He was intrusted.

One of the petitions of Agur, the Son of Jakeh, was this, "Feed me with the food that is needful for me" (Prov. xxx. 8, R.V.); and Jesus taught His disciples to pray: "Give us this day our daily bread," or, as it is in the Greek, "Give us our bread for the coming day" (St. Matt. vi. 11).

Food, bread, meat: these are emblems of the means of physical sustenance. Fire without fuel expires, and the body without nutrition will die. But let a heroic soul become the subject of enthusiasm and passion, and it will be seen that he rises for a time superior to the cravings of appetite and the necessities of the bodily frame. Let the mind be unduly depressed by pain and sorrow, and fasting will be easy and natural. Darius could not eat when his favourite minister of state was in the lion's den. David could not partake of food when his child died. In like manner, when our souls are stirred we forget the claims of the flesh.

The patriarch of Uz cherished the Oracles of God with such loving zeal and passionate attachment that he said, "I have treasured up the words of His mouth more than my necessary food" (Job xxiii. 12, R.V.).

When our 33rd Regiment was nearing Magdala, they had marched for hours over burning plains under a scorching sky without water or rest, and the heat began to tell upon the men. Many were ready to fall down from exhaustion, when suddenly the sharp cracking of the rifles told our soldiers that the foe was in the front and the fighting had begun. Hunger, thirst, fatigue were completely forgotten in the eagerness and intensity of their desire for the fray. Christ came not to destroy, but to save; not to redden the earth with blood, but to adorn it with the beauty of love and holiness. His object was the noblest imaginable; and when He saw any signs of progress towards the accomplishment of His Father's design, He was delighted. When He saw the people moved with concern respecting their relationship to Him, He was stirred to the depths of His being with mighty enthusiasm, which made Him oblivious of the sense of physical need.

> For when the power of imparting joy
> Is equal to the will, the human soul
> Requires no other Heaven.

May we imbibe His spirit and emulate His example! "Let this mind be in you, which was in Christ Jesus." May we find our nourishment, refreshment, and invigoration in the service of God and man.

IX.

Ripe for the Reapers.

There is a day in spring
When under all the earth, the secret germs
Begin to stir and glow before they bud.
The wealth and festal pomps of midsummer
Lie in the heart of that inglorious hour,
Which no man names with blessing, tho' its
    work
Is blessed by all the world. Such days there
    are
In the slow story of the growth of souls.

Saviour ! what might be Thy musings ?
    What the yearnings of Thy breast ?
(Which alone Thy Father knew of)
    As Thy weary frame did rest ?
There before Thee lay the city,
    Fig and olive clustering fair ;
Oh, the anguish ! Oh, the pity !
    For the blinded sinners there !

Ripe for the Reapers.

"Say not ye, There are yet four months, and then cometh
the harvest? Behold, I say unto you, Lift up your eyes,
and look on the fields, that they are white already unto
harvest."—St. John iv. 35.

THROUGHOUT the conversations by the
well of Sychar, as He so often did elsewhere
and at other times, Christ used the most familiar
objects of nature as vehicles of spiritual instruction. At almost every point, however, His similes
and symbols receive, both from the woman of
Samaria and from His own disciples, a cold,
hard, and literal interpretation. (*a*) He speaks
of the provisions of the Gospel in their freeness,
preciousness, and adaptation to human need.
She thinks of the water in the well only. (*b*)
He refers to spiritual nutrition. They think of

that food which satisfies the cravings of the body. (c) His mind is absorbed in the contemplation of the possibilities and issues which will accrue speedily from the widespread interest created amongst the multitude by the testimony of the woman. They think of the natural harvest only, and " four months " must elapse before that comes. The vale of Shechem, famous for its fields of grain, lay stretched before their eyes in the tender green of their first sprouting. But He is not speaking of the natural, but of the spiritual, harvest. The crowds are coming in the distance. Their garments are white. As Christ and His disciples were seated on a slight elevation, they could observe the people coming from the city towards them thus arrayed. " Say not ye," etc.

If these words were appropriate and telling when uttered by Him on that occasion, they are still more applicable to the need of the world and the duty of the Church to-day, and the lapse of time has not diminished, but increased, their force and truth. Note

I. THAT THERE ARE ENCOURAGING FACTS WHICH LEAD US TO BELIEVE THAT THE WORLD IS PREPARED FOR A MIGHTY RELIGIOUS MOVEMENT.

"The fields . . . are white already unto harvest."

These signs of the times, these indications of the powerful working of the Divine Spirit upon the consciences of our fellow-men, are utterly unnoticed by dull sense, and unseen by blind unbelief; they are noted and appreciated only by those whose spiritual perceptions are quick, and whose zeal is as a flame of fire. To those who are lethargic in spirit, under the influence of worldliness and doubt, the harvest is always "four months" distant; but to those whose souls glow with the expanding love of the Master, who share His feelings and look out upon the world with His eyes of compassion, "the fields are white already." Let us be thankful for multiplied facilities for the spread of Divine Truth.

(*a*) *Doors once closed are now open.*

It is not a long time ago that many countries were opposed to the introduction of the Word of

God. Twenty-five years since, Dr. Lewis entered
Rome, and his pocket Bible was taken from him.
In 1895 he went again, and found forty-seven
thousand copies of the Holy Book circulated in
the city. Even now there are in some parts
of Continental Europe lingering vestiges of the
old spirit of tyranny and intolerance. Let us
hope that they will quickly disappear, and that
rapid progress will be made towards the enjoy-
ment of liberty in every land under the sun. It
is useless to prohibit the dissemination of the
Word of God. As well might Canute command
the tide to advance no further.

The daughter of the Mayor of Baune once lost
her canary, and her wise father issued strict
orders that all the gates of the town should be
closed, lest the bird should escape. Are there
any places whose gates are closed against the
Bible? They may forbid and prohibit its admission, but the Truth ignores the injunctions of
parliaments and councils, of priests and popes.
It refuses to be circumscribed within any limited
area. It flies on the wings of the wind—which
are infinitely fleeter and faster than those of
any bird—and soars and sings in unfettered

freedom.   There was a time when it was right to pray—

> Open a door which earth and hell
> May strive to shut, but strive in vain.

That time has passed away ; and now it is our duty to express our indebtedness to a beneficent Providence for supplying us with ever-multiplying opportunities for the distribution of the Scriptures. In one of the most rousing hymns which we sometimes sing we recognise the greatness of the change.

> Sons of God, your Saviour praise,
> He the door hath opened wide,
> He hath given the Word of grace :
> Jesu's Word is glorified.

It is a most encouraging fact that

(*b*) *The Bible is translated into more than three hundred of the languages of the world.*

This is a work which has been mainly accomplished within the last century.   There can be no reaping without sowing ; and there can be no sowing unless the seed is transferred into the right basket, ready to be scattered.   The seed is the Word of God, the basket is the language into which it is translated.   This is what Dr. Morrison did for China, Dr. Carey for India, Robert Moffat for Great Namaqualand in South Africa, John Hunt for Fiji : they transferred the incorruptible Seed from one basket to another.

The magnificent results achieved in this direction have been brought about mainly through the agency of the British and Foreign Bible Society. This is one of the most beneficent institutions in existence : its bases are broad and catholic ; its help is generously given to all missionaries, irrespective of creed and sect, first in the translation of the inspired volume into the vernacular of the tribe, and then in its circulation ; and the Pentecostal miracle is reproduced in a form consonant with the order of nature, *i.e.* we may hear all tribes speak, in the peculiar dialect in which they were born, the mighty works of God. Another inspiring fact is this—

(*c*) *Humanity longs for God.*

It is quite evident that such a feeling exists, and that men for whom Christ died are everywhere longing for a power that will free them from sin. How true is this ! Abroad there is growing discontent with ancient superstitions, and an intense desire for the Gospel of Jesus.

As the eye was made for light, the ear for sound, the lungs for air, so the soul of man was made for God. There is a religious faculty in him which finds its development and satisfaction only in fellowship with his Creator, Preserver, and Redeemer.

> Held our eyes no sunny sheen,
> How could sunshine e'er be seen !
> Dwelt no power Divine within us,
> How could God's Divineness win us !

In the most degraded pagan there is the Godward instinct. Weakened by neglect and debased by idolatrous surroundings, often it asserts its existence and wails forth its woe, like an infant, peevish and restless, because bereft of his mother, and ceases not to cry until lifted into her arms and clasped to her bosom. The child cannot tell the cause of his distress, and the heathen may not be able to render any rational explanation of his discontent, but just like a babe losing all sorrow and gaining all joy in the loving embrace of mother, so the moment you preach Jesus to the heathen, he recognises in Him the realisation of his deepest need and intensest desires.

In the depths of Central Africa a forlorn
woman was discovered by one of the missionaries.
When Christ was presented to her mind, she is
reported to have broken out into demonstrations
of delight, saying, "Oh, that is He who has come
to me so often in my prayers! I could not find
who He was." Longfellow enshrines this thought
in his "Hiawatha" when he sings—

> Ye whose hearts are fresh and simple,
> Who have faith in God and nature,
> Who believe that in all the ages,
> Every human heart is human;
> That in even savage bosoms
> There are longings, yearnings, strivings,
> For the good they comprehend not;
> That the feeble hands and helpless,
> Groping blindly in the darkness,
> Touch God's right hand in that darkness,
> And are lifted up and strengthened.

The Macedonian cry, "Come over and help us,"
reaches us from many lands; and it should sound
in our ears like a clarion call to pray more
earnestly, to give more liberally, and to work
more earnestly for the universal spread of the
kingdom of Jesus.

Young Hindus are seeking the benefits of an English education by the thousands: some of them come to our universities and colleges; others in increasing numbers are being taught in missionary schools in India. The influence of our literature already permeates that vast empire. What is the result? With the influx of Western ideas there is a gradual decay of confidence in their ancestral beliefs and habits. Their minds are unsettled by the intrusion of doubt and uncertainty. If we disturb their faith in their old religions, surely it becomes our plain duty to tell them of Him whose name is above every other name, and whose peace is a panacea for their woe. Let me remind you that the Queen of Great Britain is the Empress of India, and in that continent the subjects of the British Crown number as many as the inhabitants of Russia, Prussia, France, and Austria united—about three hundred millions. Let those grim evils, famine and plague, decimate their numbers and desolate their homes, and before long Great Britain sends its munificent contribution of more than half a million pounds for the relief of the sufferers. If we are so ready to give temporal, shall we

withhold spiritual, help? Do you not hear their
cry?

> From many an ancient river,
> From many a palmy plain,
> They call us to deliver
> Their land from error's chain?

Missionaries inform us in their recent reports
that this is literally true — the heathen are
clamouring for the Bread of Life, they are
entreating the servants of Jesus to come and
proclaim to them the glad tidings of salvation.

> Far and wide, though all unknowing,
> Pants for Thee each human breast;
> Human tears for Thee are flowing,
> Human hearts in Thee would rest.
> Thirsting as for dews of even,
> As the new-mown grass for rain,
> Thee they seek as God of Heaven,
> Thee as man for sinners slain.

> Saviour, lo! the isles are waiting,
> Stretched the hand and strained the sight
> For Thy Spirit, new creating,
> . Love's pure flame and wisdom's light.
> Give the Word, and of the preacher
> Speed the foot and touch the tongue,
> Till on earth by every creature
> Glory to the Lamb be sung.

It is quite evident

II. THAT IT IS OUR DUTY TO STUDY THE SIGNIFICANCE AND PROMOTE THE SUCCESS OF ANY MOVEMENT AMONG THE PEOPLE TOWARDS JESUS.

"Lift up your eyes and look on the fields," etc. Hengstenberg says that when Jesus spoke these words, He pointed to the approaching Samaritans. That was the harvest of which He spoke, and for which He longed. It was not one that would take place at a distant time, but one to be reaped in the actual present. Dr. Plummer tells us that "in the green blades just showing through the soil the faith of the sower sees the white ears that will soon be there. So also, in the flocking of these ignorant Samaritans to Him for instruction Christ sees the abundant harvest of souls that is to follow." It was then spring-time in nature, and therefore seed-time, and the average length of the interval between this season and the harvest was "four months." After diligently sowing the seed, the husbandman waits patiently for the grain to grow and ripen, and then he reaps. But in the spiritual world there are no limitations as to time. The seed of life, sown by Himself and by the woman of Samaria, had already brought forth fruit, for the inhabitants of the city of Sychar were coming in large numbers, guided by her who so recently had received the light and peace of the Gospel. God can save at any time—summer and winter, spring and autumn. Whenever there is need for His help, His hand is not shortened that it cannot save; whenever there is a cry or a sigh for deliverance, His ear is not heavy that it cannot hear. There are, however, special seasons of awakening, when a tidal wave of blessing sweeps over the land. Lowell says—

> Once to every man and nation comes the moment to
> decide,
> In the strife of truth with falsehood, for the good or
> evil side.

Yes, and more than once. He comes often, and works mightily upon the consciences of persons and communities. On such occasions it is for the watchmen of Zion or the representatives of the Church of God to note the trend of events, and to be like men of Issachar, who "had understanding of the times to know what Israel ought to do" (I Chron. xii. 32)

God intends us to be reapers as well as sowers. To sow requires strong faith ; to reap, patience. It is said that the task of ingathering is more difficult now because the people are accustomed to the solemn warnings and the tender entreaties of the Gospel. Should we not regard it as more easy now, because of the preparatory work done by those faithful husbandmen who toiled in the heat and the labour of their day, and who have exchanged the sickle for the palm of victory? They broke up the fallow ground, ploughed the soil, and sowed the seed, and they have not worked in vain. The influences of the Good Spirit have descended as the sun and the rain upon the earth, like healing and fertilising blessings, for the enrichment of the soil and the growth of germs. The fields are now white. Let the golden grain be gathered safely into the garner of God.

" I sent you to reap that whereon ye bestowed no labour: other men laboured, and ye are entered into their labours " (ver. 38). The joy and honour of the harvest are to be shared alike by both sower and reaper. There is to be no monopoly on the part of either. Dr. Dixon illustrated this thought of the obligation of

present workers to their predecessors, by imagining a ripe ear of corn saying to its root, "What a
miserable thing you are down there in the mud!"
But the root modestly replied, "Yes, but what
would you have been but for me?" "And he
that reapeth receiveth wages and gathereth fruit
unto life eternal, that both he that soweth and he
that reapeth may rejoice together" (ver. 36).

The Church of God is gaining proficiency in
sowing, but is she studying the art of reaping?
Our fathers were honoured by God in being
instrumental in His hands of gathering in on a
large scale: they were successful reapers. Are
we seeking fitness for this work?

To the eye of Jesus the world was composed of
so many fields covered with precious corn ripe for
the reapers, *i.e.* teeming with souls to be brought
to Him. What He required were men who could
wield the sickle with skill. To Him the time to
reap was not the distant future, but the living
present. "The harvest truly is great, but the
labourers are few: pray ye, therefore, the Lord of
the harvest that He would thrust labourers into
His harvest" (St. Luke x. 2).

As He bade His disciples "lift up their eyes on

the fields," He reminds us of the duty which devolves upon us in relation to the surging masses surrounding our sanctuaries. For the moment we look, but it is through the coloured glasses of prejudice and pride; and we are apt to say of them, as the Jews said of the Samaritans, "those people are heathens, dogs." Let us gaze upon them through the medium of common sympathy, and remember that all of them have souls, God-created, blood-bought, and deathless. Jesus had compassion on the multitude. This is the main reason why the common people heard Him gladly. He knew the secret of reaching the masses. He loved them, and they felt it to be so. It is true that He went to Temple and synagogue to expound the Law and proclaim the Gospel. He went also to those who were outside these sacred places of worship, and published the love of God on the mountain and by the sea.

John Wesley preached in the churches of this land until he was prohibited. At the time, the prohibition was regarded as an unmitigated calamity; but now, after the lapse of a century, it is felt to be the greatest blessing that could have come to the famed evangelist and his followers.

What was the result? Denied the use of the pulpits of the Established Church, he was compelled to deliver his message to the democracy—to the colliers of Kingswood, the miners of Cornwall, and the weavers of Lancashire. The Rev. W. L. Watkinson once said that to-day statesmen and politicians are running after the butterfly, the working-man, but that John Wesley went after him when the butterfly was only a caterpillar, *i.e.* when the working-man had no vote, no franchise, and few, if any, of the advantages he has now. In the spirit of love let us " lift up our eyes and look on the fields, for they are white already to harvest." Let us hail the approach of the people to Jesus: let us help them by word and deed. Let us lay aside every vestige of prejudice and pride, and cultivate tender sympathy with those who are seeking Him.

> Enlarge, inflame, and fill my heart
>   With boundless charity divine ;
> So shall I all my strength exert,
>   And love them with a zeal like Thine.
> And lead them to Thy open side,
>   The sheep for whom the Shepherd died.

X.

The Faith of Experience.

There is but one chance of life in admitting so far the possibility of the Christian verity, as to try it on its own merits. There is not the slightest possibility of finding whether it be true or not first. "Show me a sign first, and I will come," you say. "No," answers God. "Come first, and you shall see the sign."—RUSKIN.

Ten minutes spent in Christ's society every day, ay, two minutes, if it be face to face and heart to heart, will make the whole life different.
—DRUMMOND.

The Faith of Experience.

"Now we believe, not because of thy saying : for we have heard Him ourselves, and know that this is indeed the Christ, the Saviour of the world."—ST. JOHN iv. 42.

THE history of the Samaritans is replete with interest. In the early ages the central province, like the rest of Palestine, was inhabited by the Israelites. About the year 709 B.C. Esarhaddon, King of Assyria, son of and successor to Sennacherib, having gathered together a great army, marched into the Holy Land, and took captive all those who were the remnants of the former Captivity (except a few who had escaped into the mountains), and carried them away into Babylon and Assyria. By this system of general and compulsory emigration, the country, once so fair and beautiful, was in danger of becoming utterly desolate through lack of inhabitants. In order to populate it once again, he sent colonists from Babylon, Cuthah, Ava, Hamath, and Sepharvaim, and established them in the cities of Samaria. On settling in their new home, they found that the country was infested with lions. Thinking that the ravages of these ferocious animals was a scourge sent by the god of the land, the Assyrian king ordered a captive Hebrew priest to go back to the colonists, with a view to instruct them in the religion of the country. Notwithstanding this circumstance, they did not cast off the worship of the deities of the provinces whence they came, and the result was that their religion became a hybrid and monstrous mixture of pagan polytheism and Jewish monotheism. "So these nations feared the Lord, and served their graven images" (2 Kings xvii. 41).

In this state they continued for three hundred years, *i.e.* until the temple was erected on Mount Gerizim about 409 B.C. ; and even then, although they were led to adopt many Jewish customs and dogmas, they were still a long way from the orthodox belief and practice. One peculiar feature of the Samaritan creed was this, that of the Old Testament documents the Pentateuch alone was recognised as the Divinely-appointed authority for the regulation of their life; they repudiated the other portions, probably from a fear lest they should discover to their sorrow that, after all [their reverence for Gerizim, Jerusalem was the place where worship was to be presented and festivals to be celebrated. Let us note carefully that those who are represented in this text as saying "we believe," were once semi-sceptics: they are now believers. In a short time they emerged out of a state of comparative ignorance and unbelief into the light and rest of faith, and underwent an important crisis in their mental and spiritual history. How did they rise to this state? By two agencies, the saying of the woman of Samaria, and their personal application to the Christ. We learn

I. The Value of Testimony.

In the thirty-ninth verse of this chapter the recognition of the work she did is distinct and honourable. "And from that city many of the Samaritans believed on Him, because of the word

of the woman, who testified, He told me all
things that ever I did" (R.V.). During the interview with Jesus at the well, such great impressions
were produced on her mind that she left her waterpot and ran into the city. He forgot His three-
fold want—hunger, thirst, fatigue. If we imagine
Him as hearing the groans of a struggling spirit
whilst in the act of making a new planet, He
would pause in the work of creation, if necessary,
to help a soul in distress. As He became oblivious
of His physical necessities, she was so entranced
by His words that she left her waterpot at the
well, and hastened with joyful certainty and with
burning zeal to be His herald. The successive
stages marking her spiritual progress may be placed
under three heads—she heard, she felt, she spoke.
This is an order of procedure which is not un-
common, but typical of what occurs in the life of
thousands. Let the heart experience the glow
and gladness of Divine love, and soon the tongue
will tell the marvels of Redeeming Grace. Well
might the Psalmist say, " My heart was hot within
me; while I was musing the fire kindled : then
spake I with my tongue" (Ps. xxxix. 3). As
direct and outspoken testimony is a suitable

expression and an effectual preservative of our religious life, so also does it become an indispensable necessity to the advancement of the Saviour's kingdom. To this agency, accompanied by the blessing of God, and vitalised by His Spirit, is to be attributed the phenomenal growth of the Christian religion throughout the Roman Empire during the first three centuries. Then every disciple was a missionary, a witness-bearer; and in their case ancient prophecy was literally fulfilled: "They shall speak of the glory of Thy kingdom, and talk of Thy power" (Ps. cxlv. 11). The ardour of their zeal was not quenched, not even cooled, by angry persecution; but, like the action of wind on fire, it became more intense and fervid.

Two of His apostles, John and Peter, were on one occasion arraigned before the Sanhedrin. They were two very different men in their temperaments: the one, gentle, mild, the disciple whom Jesus loved; the other, rough, impetuous, boisterous, but not the Peter who denied his Lord thrice, and followed Him afar off; since then he has undergone a complete transformation—he is a new creature. The head and front of their offending was, that they had been speaking and

preaching in the name of their Master. They
remembered that He had taught them to regard
testimony as a duty and a privilege, and promised
that, when placed in positions of peril and difficulty,
He would inspire them with right words to utter.
Is there a conflict in their minds, or any hesitation
as to which course to take? Is it to be a cowardly
suppression or a brave and manly avowal of their
new views? Whatever was the difference in their
temperament, they both united in saying to the
Sanhedrin : "Whether it be right in the sight of
God to hearken unto you rather than unto God,
judge ye: for we cannot but speak the things
which we saw and heard" (Acts iv. 19, R.V.).
When Martin Luther realised that justification
was not by deeds of penance not by gifts of
money, nor by priestly absolution, but by a simple
trust of the penitent soul in the mercy of God
through the death of Jesus ; when he stood before
the Diet of Worms, in the presence of Charles V.,
cardinals, archbishops, and priests, a cynical and
august assembly, he did not shrink from declaring
his convictions, but uttered those memorable
words : "*Here I stand. I cannot do otherwise.
God help me. Amen.*"

When the three Oxford University men, John and Charles Wesley and George Whitefield, learnt the way of God more perfectly, *i.e.* that salvation was not by works only, but by faith showing itself in holy deeds, they did not keep the secret locked up in their own bosoms; they did not practise any reticence or reserve, and think it wrong to disclose the privacy of their sacred convictions. They had found the priceless Treasure, and thought it their duty to make it known through the length and breadth of the land. Wherever they went their cry was—

> What we have felt and seen,
> With confidence we tell;
> And publish to the sons of men
> The signs infallible.

Luther testified: hence the Reformation of the sixteenth century. John Wesley and his coadjutors testified: hence the Evangelical Revival of the last century. This nameless Samaritan woman testified, and "many believed on Him." So if we utter a few simple, heartfelt words for His glory, we cannot tell what may be the result.

To rely, however, upon human testimony is

not always absolutely safe. It may be correct, as in the case before us ; but it may be also unreliable, as in the instance of the ten spies who brought a false report of "the land flowing with milk and honey." We need a safer rule ; and this leads us to consider

II. The Superior Value of Experience.

" Now we believe, not because of thy speaking : for we have heard Him for ourselves, and know that this is indeed the Saviour of the world " (R.V.).

In many secular affairs this rule holds good : the most valuable and permanent knowledge springs from, not hearsay but observation ; not testimony, but experience.

To understand the science of chemistry, it is not enough to read books and hear lectures on the subject : its theories must be reduced to, and tested by, a series of experiments. Religion is the science of noble living ; and in order to perceive its utility and beauty, it is necessary to obtain experimental and practical acquaintance with its truths. " If any man willeth to do His will, he shall know of the teaching, whether it be of God, or whether I speak from Myself." (St. John vii. 17, R.V.).

Multitudes fail to comply with this recognised canon by which the reality of any Divine revelation is to be authenticated. They read other books, instead of reading the Bible; they form their opinions from the dicta of others, instead of making a direct and personal application to the Lord Jesus Christ; they drink of the streams, which are sometimes polluted, instead of going to the Source. To such we say, " Be just, be honourable; do not affirm that Jesus never existed but in the poetic imagination of His followers, and that His Gospel is a cunningly-devised fable, before you have complied with this rule." As rational were it for the student of chemistry to pronounce an adverse opinion on that science before he has made any experiments, as it is for agnostics to dogmatise on spiritual religion before they have applied the only test. One hour spent in holy converse with Christ secures a larger accession to our store of true religion than a whole lifetime engaged in listening to the testimonies of others, be the witnesses never so true and eloquent. It is not subtle arguing, bold imagining or philosophic theorising, that secures admission into the kingdom of God, but a personal faith in a living, ever-loving Saviour. A little girl was so ill that her disease had taken away her eyesight. She was asked "Are you quite blind?" "Yes," she said, "I am quite blind; but I can see Jesus with the eye of my heart." Happy child: she understood the simple yet sublime philosophy of saving faith. No wonder that Jesus should break forth into an outburst of praise as He thought of the ways of God. "I thank Thee, O Father, Lord of heaven and earth, that Thou didst hide these things from the wise and understanding, and didst reveal them unto babes: yea, Father for so it was well-pleasing in Thy sight" (Matt. xi. 25, R.V.).

The Queen of Sheba had heard of the wealth of Solomon's treasury and the surpassing greatness of his wisdom; but she did not believe until she came to his palace and saw its magnificence, beheld the king himself and listened to his words. She then acknowledged the truth of the rumours she had heard, and said, "Howbeit I believed not the words, until I came, and mine eyes had seen it; and, behold, the half was not told me : thy wisdom and prosperity exceedeth the fame which I heard " (1 Kings x. 7).

In Christian England there are thousands who have heard much more of the King of Glory than the Queen of Sheba ever heard of Solomon. Pictures of Bible scenes were in their hands as early as their toys; the first story which charmed their childhood was that of the Manger; and their familiarity with Scripture narratives and Gospel truth increased as they advanced into youth, and matured into manhood. They repair to the house of God regularly, and listen to His servant respectfully, but their hearts are not glowing with love to the great King—they are benumbed with the cold of unbelief. We should like to say to them : Do not be content with reading of Jesus in the Bible and in good books, nor with hearing of Him in sermons from the pulpit and addresses from the Sunday-school desk. Deal with Him as the Queen of Sheba did with Solomon. Come to Him : behold with your own eyes the treasures of His grace, hear with your own ears the matchless music of His voice; and as with Sheba's Queen, so it will be with you—your unbelief will melt away in His presence like the thawing of ice under the heat of the sun; the truth of the report given by minister, teacher, or parent will be not only confirmed, but surpassed by the glory and blessedness of the actual realisation of His favour. Once you enter into the Royal Palace, listen to the voice and gaze upon the face of the King who is infinitely greater than Solomon, your faith will rest, not on testimony, but experience; not report, but conviction. You will have to exclaim, like the Samaritans, "This is indeed the Christ, the Saviour of the world."

PRINTED BY
MORRISON AND GIBB LIMITED, EDINBURGH.